STARTUP SPIRIT: NURTURING ENTREPRENEURSHIP IN KASHMIR

DR SAIMA PAUL

Dedicated to my Parents, Family and Teachers

Contents

FOREWORD

I am thrilled to have the opportunity to compose the foreword for "**Startup Spirit: Nurturing Entrepreneurship in Kashmir**", a book by Dr. Saima Paul that provides a perceptive examination of entrepreneurship in the region. Dr. Paul's research is a critical contribution to the comprehension of the distinctive opportunities and challenges that entrepreneurs encounter in Kashmir.

The book commences by delineating the modern definition of entrepreneurship, emphasizing the characteristics and perspectives of successful entrepreneurs, and elucidating the importance of businesses in the context of economic expansion. Dr. Paul subsequently guides readers through the startup process, from the initial idea to its successful execution, providing practical guidance on the development of business models, validating business ideas, and conceptualizing. For individuals who are contemplating the establishment of a business, these sections offer indispensable insights.

Dr. Paul also explores the startup ecosystem, underscoring the significance of funding, networking, incubators, and accelerators. She emphasizes the potential of technology and digital tools to create new opportunities for businesses in Kashmir, providing practical strategies for utilizing innovation to drive growth.

The book's emphasis on Kashmir as a land with untapped potential is a significant virtue. Dr. Paul investigates the socio-economic and cultural factors that influence entrepreneurship in the region, while simultaneously identifying industries such as agribusiness, tourism, handicrafts, and fashion that present promising growth prospects. She also addresses the potential of contemporary marketing strategies and technology to revitalize conventional sectors, such as agribusiness and handicrafts.

Lastly, Dr. Paul addresses the obstacles associated with the establishment and expansion of enterprises in Kashmir, offering strategies for surmounting socio-political impediments and cultivating resilience. The Startup Spirit is a comprehensive and empowering guide for aspiring entrepreneurs in Kashmir, providing valuable insights for anyone who aspires to contribute to the region's economic development and innovation.

Dr. Ganzanfer
Associate professor
Floriculture
SKUAST-Kashmir

PREFACE

The increasing acknowledgment of entrepreneurship's capacity to stimulate economic growth and creativity has resulted in heightened emphasis on the crucial function of startups in societal transformation. Communities and regions are perpetually seeking innovative strategies to cultivate entrepreneurial spirit, especially in developing markets such as Kashmir. With appropriate assistance and chances, entrepreneurs—particularly in areas with unexploited potential—can serve as a significant catalyst for change. Aspiring entrepreneurs in Kashmir encounter distinct hurdles, primarily due to socio-political variables and resource constraints that frequently impede advancement.

Current study indicates that promoting entrepreneurship benefits not only individual entrepreneurs but also contributes to the broader development of the community and economy. Entrepreneurs drive job creation, innovation, and sustainability, and the subsequent impact of their achievement advantages those in their vicinity. This comprehension has propelled considerable academic and practical initiatives focused on fostering entrepreneurship, particularly in areas such as Kashmir, where the entrepreneurial environment is undergoing fast transformation.

Research indicates that areas with a robust entrepreneurial ecosystem experience significant economic expansion, enhanced social mobility, and elevated quality of life. Equipping entrepreneurs with appropriate tools—education, resources, and opportunities—can facilitate the realization of their full potential. Furthermore, these entrepreneurs are predisposed to establish inclusive and resilient enterprises that enhance their communities and foster greater societal transformation. Consequently, it is essential to investigate the determinants of entrepreneurship in these locations and formulate methods to tackle their specific issues.

Startup Spirit: Fostering Entrepreneurshipin Kashmir represents a substantial addition to the examination of entrepreneurship within this environment. The book aims to examine the various aspects of entrepreneurship, the challenges encountered by entrepreneurs, and the techniques to surmount them. Dr. Saima Paul provides a comprehensive examination of the interplay between innovation, technology, and cultural influences in shaping the entrepreneurial environment in Kashmir. This book seeks to enhance the development of a dynamic and sustainable entrepreneurial ecosystem, thereby fostering a successful and inclusive future for the region.

Dr Saima Paul

Acknowledgements

With true I thank the **Almighty** that has showered me with blessing and grace to complete this piece of work.

I would also like to express my gratefulness for my **parents and family** for their support and love.

I want to thank Hourable **Prof. (Dr.) Nazir Ahmad Ganai (Hon'ble Vice Chancellor, SKUAST-Kashmir)** for his support, guidance and motivation.

I would also like to thank **Dr. Naveed (CEO, SKIIE Centre, SKUAST-Kashmir)** and **Dr. Malik Raies ul Islam (Assistant Professor, Animal science, SKUAST-Kashmir)** for their support.

Dr. Saima Paul

Prologue

Often referred to as "Paradise on Earth," Kashmir is an area complete with unrealized promise rather than only one with breathtaking scenery and energetic culture. Underneath its gorgeous exterior is a territory ready for development, and here, the worldwide tide of enterprise is beginning to settle. Among the young people of Kashmir, a growing community of inventors, artists, and problem-solvers has developed in recent years. They are empowering themselves by accepting the startup ecosystem as a potent tool for social transformation, economic resilience, and self-reliance.

For young people from Kashmir, the disruptions in traditional sectors and the obstacles to conventional employment have spurred a notable change toward entrepreneurship. They see startups as a road toward empowerment and optimism for the future, not only as commercial endeavours. Young Kashmiris are grabbing the chance to develop answers that meet local needs and simultaneously satisfy global ambitions in technology, travel, fashion, or agriculture. This shift is about creating a vibrant entrepreneurial environment capable of driving good change throughout the region, not only about launching enterprises.

For those who want to join this movement, this book, **Startup Spirit: Fostering Entrepreneurship in Kashmir,** offers both a manual and motivation. It provides a thorough view of entrepreneurship ideas catered to Kashmir's unique situation. UsingThrough pragmatic guidance, actual case studies, and actionable recommendations, readers will be thoroughly aware of what it takes to flourish in the startup environment. From first idea generation and validation to scaling and worldwide expansion, every chapter examines a different facet of the startup path.

The book starts with defining entrepreneurship in the contemporary environment and investigates the qualities and attitudes that make effective modern entrepreneurs. It discusses why startups are essential for economic development and how they could spur innovation and employment creation in Kashmir. From there, it advances to doable actions for realizing ideas—verifying company concepts, developing business models, and creating engaging value propositions.

Knowing the tools and networks in the startup ecosystem is essential. Hence, the book looks at the function of accelerators, incubators, and finance sources. It also emphasizes the need for networking and chances for cooperation, as well as how digital tools and technology may be used to propel company expansion.

The book primarily focuses on Kashmir itself, its unique possibilities and difficulties. It explores the socioeconomic scene, cultural quirks, and geographical elements influencing regional entrepreneurship. It addresses the requirement of policies honouring cultural preservation while promoting economic development and the necessity of flexible approaches bridging history and modernity for success.

The book offers focused advice in several industries where Kashmir has a clear competitive advantage—agribusiness and agri-tech, tourism, handicrafts, fashion, and technology. It looks at possibilities in saffron and apple farming, eco-tourism, traditional crafts like Pashmina, and digital-first company models that profit from worldwide remote work trends. Case studies of fashion businesses, creative tourism projects, and successful agriculture startups highlight the possibilities for success in various fields.

A significant component of entrepreneurship is overcoming obstacles and maintaining progress. The book examines risk management techniques, resilience building, and sociopolitical uncertainty. It addresses how to negotiate the complexity of developing a company from local to global, offers ideas for comprehending foreign markets, creates strategic alliances, and adjusts business models to fit many cultural settings.

Startup Spirit: Fostering Entrepreneurship in Kashmir, nurturing entrepreneurship in the region is not only a manual for starting companies. It motivates individuals to welcome entrepreneurial energy, maximize their creative ability, and help the local economy to be rebuilt. Entrepreneurs in Kashmir can remove obstacles, seize possibilities, and create a legacy of sustainable development and wealth by combining local knowledge with a worldwide vision.

I

Entrepreneurship and Startups

Entrepreneurship

Entrepreneurship is starting, growing, and running a new company endeavour in search of profit. As business owners spot market prospects and turn ideas into workable business plans, it captures the essence of creativity and risk-taking. The core of entrepreneurship is its capacity to create value using newly introduced goods or services to satisfy consumer wants. Entrepreneurs are often viewed as change agents promoting economic growth by generating jobs, boosting competitiveness, and supporting technical developments.

Essential components of entrepreneurship

- Entrepreneurs use their imagination to create original answers to challenges or enhance current items.
- Starting a business entails financial risks, so entrepreneurs must be ready to commit their funds and deal with uncertainty.
- Vision: Effective business owners have a clear idea for their company, and market trends are clearly visible to them.
- They must adequately allocate capital, labour, technology, and resources to meet their company goals.
- Small local businesses and big companies can all show the manifestation of entrepreneurship. It covers many sectors and goes beyond technology or high-growth companies.

Entrepreneurship encompasses all activities undertaken by an individual to start and manage entrepreneurial ventures in alignment with evolving social, political, and economic contexts. Entrepreneurship involves anticipating consumer preferences, emotions, behaviours, tastes, and trends and launching business enterprises to fulfil these consumer expectations. Entrepreneurship is regarded as a 'new product' that allows businesspeople to create innovative organizational structures and engage in novel economic activities that address the evolving demands of society. The loosening of cultural rigidities is primarily attributable to this new phenomenon, ' entrepreneurship.' Entrepreneurship is the capacity of entrepreneurs to evaluate risks and create precarious enterprises yet align seamlessly with the evolving economic landscape. What is entrepreneurship? The term 'entrepreneurship' encompasses numerous definitions. Upon thoroughly examining all accessible options, we find that entrepreneurship constitutes a strategy for conducting business that capitalizes on opportunities present within a market. Self-employment requires the utilization of all available chances within the economic system to establish and operate new enterprises. A prospective entrepreneur must demonstrate a willingness to pursue investment possibilities in the market to manage the firm based on discernible prospects effectively.

Entrepreneurial mindset

- An entrepreneurial mindset denotes a particular mental condition that directs human behaviour toward entrepreneurial endeavours and results. People with entrepreneurial mindsets often find themselves drawn to opportunities, innovation, and creating new value. Traits encompass the capacity to undertake calculated risks and embrace the realities of change and uncertainty.
- The traditional career path is no longer relevant. According to a survey commissioned by Intuit, statistics indicate that 40 to 50 per cent of students who commenced college in 2016 will engage in self-employment or freelance work at some stage. The economy, student aspirations, and global expectations of students differ significantly from those I encountered upon graduating college. There is no superior method to equip students for the 21st-century landscape—whether they aim to join a giant corporation, establish their enterprise, pursue an academic career, or engage in public service than by fostering their entrepreneurial talents.

- In entrepreneurial education, the focus is on cultivating skills rather than establishing enterprises. We unequivocally support and encourage students aspiring to create the next Facebook, and MSU offers numerous resources to assist them. The objective is to cultivate interdisciplinary abilities that foster the development of an entrepreneurial attitude.
- The word encapsulates a collection of interdisciplinary life and professional competencies that characterize an individual as innovative, resourceful, and value-generating. The entrepreneurial mindset is applicable in several circumstances.
- It pertains to personnel in huge, hierarchical organizations, community organizers, academics, inventors, physicians, attorneys, politicians, musicians, and public officials. The abilities acquired are not exclusive to startup enterprises but apply to all individuals. We assert that developing an entrepreneurial attitude is an essential talent for the 21st century. Individuals who master it will succeed significantly in their jobs, regardless of their chosen path, as they inherently become inventive and adaptable.
- To master entrepreneurship, one must exercise it. It is based on experience. Like the impossibility of learning to swim in a library, one cannot comprehend the essence of entrepreneurship without firsthand experience. We are implementing programs incorporating an experiential component into our entrepreneurship and innovation curriculum.
- There is no more opportune moment for students aspiring to establish their own business than during their college years, as the costs significantly increase once they relinquish their full-time student status. Students on campus have access to resources such as the ideation centre, The Hive, an incubator known as The Hatch, and mentors, support, and funding. Establishing a business is challenging, and the majority do not succeed. However, this is not the primary issue. The crux is that through effort, students cultivate talents that yield substantial benefits throughout their careers—in my experience, spanning decades. The rationale lies in the experience rather than the result.

Consequently, after examining the aforementioned obligations of an entrepreneur, the term 'entrepreneurship' is ultimately defined as a function including several roles, including:
· Establishing companies.

- Facilitating self-employment
- Leveraging available resources
- Implementing innovation in the original concept
- Integrating various aspects of production in a concrete manner

Entrepreneurs

Entrepreneurs can identify and perceive the presence of business opportunities in various situations. They will leverage these chances to develop new items by implementing innovative production techniques across multiple markets. They will operate in diverse ways, utilizing distinct resources to yield profit. It is essential to recognize that while most entrepreneurial ventures commence at a modest size, the proprietors of these enterprises are not necessarily limited to small-scale ownership. They are substantial business proprietors who initially assess the market before making significant investments. Small business proprietors fear danger; nonetheless, successful entrepreneurs exhibit significant innovation and possess the acumen to operate profitably in a high-risk business climate.

Innovation is essential for entrepreneurs; it is a weapon that enables them to obtain a competitive advantage over established market players. Entrepreneurs are individuals or groups who engage in entrepreneurial activities grounded in their innovative methods for addressing real-world issues.

Innovative Entrepreneurs: Their primary focus is introducing innovative concepts into the market, company, or nation. Innovations attract them, and they dedicate significant time and resources to research and development.

Imitating Entrepreneurs: People often refer to these individuals as 'copycats.' They scrutinize a successful system and replicate it, rectifying the shortcomings of the original business model while maintaining its efficiency. These entrepreneurs upgrade existing products or production processes and recommend adopting superior technology.

Fabian Entrepreneurs: These entrepreneurs are meticulous in their strategies and prudent in implementing modifications. They are not inclined toward impulsive actions and endeavour to avoid innovations or changes that do not align with their story.

Drone businesspeople: These are businesspeople averse to change. People regard them as 'old school.' They wish to conduct business using their conventional methods of manufacturing and systems. Such individuals ascribe pride and tradition to even antiquated business practices.

Functions of an Entrepreneur:
Technological Transformation

We designate these as behavioural roles. All entrepreneurs share comparable features and choose to pursue entrepreneurship because of the reasons or experiences shaping their perspectives. These entrepreneurs must fulfil specific roles to execute their tasks efficiently and manage a prosperous enterprise. These roles correspond to the fundamental managerial ones.

Transformative Influence of Entrepreneurship

A global appeal for an "entrepreneurial revolution" is emerging to address social and economic issues. This assertion simplistically presupposes that more entrepreneurs are needed to tackle these challenges. Augmenting the number of entrepreneurs is less imperative than motivating them to enhance their communities through growth, innovation, and social revolution. The revolution must focus on reforming modern entrepreneurial culture to improve its social consciousness.

People recognize entrepreneurs' ability to establish innovative enterprises that effectively address challenges. We must broaden this fundamental definition to view entrepreneurs as influential cultural transformation agents capable of reshaping their society. This does not imply dedicating time after work to tackle social issues. Entrepreneurs consciously incorporate social goals into their business plans to maximize individual and community benefits. It necessitates dismantling the notion that only governments and established corporations can fulfil social needs. Entrepreneurs, operating in proximity to the populace, are ideally situated to recognize and address pressing issues, such as poverty and inadequate access to healthcare and education.

Modern communities require more efficient and socially integrated methods to meet their needs. Entrepreneurs must recognize that they are securing long-term sustainability by founding new enterprises focused on generating economic success and promoting social progress. More developed nations serve as platforms for further growth and internationalization.

Indian Entrepreneurship:

With its startup ecosystem third-largest in the world, India has become a global powerhouse for entrepreneurship. Over 128,000 businesses have been identified as of April 2024, a startling increase from just 450 startups in 2016. Government programs, demographic benefits, and growing investment interest all help to drive this quick expansion.

Important Drivers of Startup Development

- **Advantage in Demographic Terms:** With a sizable fraction under thirty-five, India enjoys a young and energetic populace. This group is not only tech-savvy but also more likely to be entrepreneurial, which offers a ready environment for fresh business ideas.
- **Government Encouragement:** Using cash support, regulatory simplification, and mentoring program facilitation, initiatives such as Startup India have fostered the entrepreneurial environment. The government has identified over 140,000 companies that help generate almost 1.55 million in employment.
- With around $70 billion in total investments from 2019 to 2023, the Indian startup scene has drawn significant investment from venture capitalists and angel investors. Startups hoping to scale quickly depend on this flood of money.
- **Sectoral diversification:** Although technology-driven industries like fintech and e-commerce predominate, entrepreneurs are rapidly straying into other areas, including healthcare, agriculture, and education. This diversification increases resilience and extends the economic influence.

Obstacles Indian Startups Face

- Indian companies have various difficulties even in vibrant surroundings:
- Funding Limitations: For many business owners, especially in the early years of their operations, getting finance still presents a significant obstacle.
- Navigating complicated rules might be intimidating and could slow down development.
- Startups frequently face established companies with more resources and brand awareness to compete in the market.
- Attracting qualified staff is difficult given the rivalry from more prominent companies providing more competitive pay scales.

Kashmirian Entrepreneurship: Emerging Prospects

The entrepreneurial scene in Kashmir is changing as local young people try to use regional resources and solve socioeconomic issues with creative businesses. Though historically recognized for its agriculture and handicaps, tech-driven companies are attracting more and more attention presently.

- **Unique Context of Kashmiri Startups:** Cultural Heritage and Artisanal Crafts: Startups in Kashmir generally concentrate on using traditional crafts, including Pashmina shawls and papier-mâché art, to produce distinctive goods appealing to both local and worldwide markets.
- **Agricultural Innovation:** With items like saffron and apples, the area's abundant agrarian resources provide firms focused on horticulture possibilities. For nearby farmers, creative supply chain solutions can help to increase earnings.
- Given Kashmir's standing as a travel destination, entrepreneurs providing eco-tourism experiences or digital platforms linking visitors with local guides and services have great opportunities.

Difficulties unique to Kashmir

- **Infrastructure Restraints:** Bad infrastructure might affect market access and logistics.
- **Restricted Access to Funding:** Entrepreneurs could find it challenging to get funding because of the region's apparent hazards.

Government Projects

Through several government initiatives to offer financial support and training programs for aspirant entrepreneurs, attempts are being made to encourage entrepreneurship in Kashmir. Local talent is greatly nurtured, and a supportive ecosystem is created significantly by organizations like the Jammu and Kashmir Entrepreneurship Development Institute (JKEDI).

Driven by creativity and encouraged by government policies fostering entrepreneurship in many spheres, India's entrepreneurial scene is flourishing. In the meantime, Kashmir offers unique chances for aspiring business owners trying to use local resources while negotiating specific regional difficulties. Reflecting the dynamic character of entrepreneurship in India today, both ecosystems have great potential to help with job creation and economic growth.

Startups

A startup is a recently launched company project seeking to create a distinctive good, service, or business strategy with scalability and fast expansion potential. Unlike established companies, startups are sometimes distinguished by their creative ideas and dependence on technology to satisfy consumer needs and address challenges. Different definitions define startups as transient companies that look for scalable and repeatable business models, separating them from small enterprises usually running under established models. Usually, in its early phases of development, a startup is a particular kind of entrepreneurial endeavour. Often trying to disrupt established markets with new products or services, startups are defined by their emphasis on fast development and creativity. Unlike established companies that might focus on consistent expansion and profitability from the start, startups typically operate under uncertainty and try to verify their business ideas rapidly.

Characteristics of startups

- High Potential for Growth: Startups, generally aiming for big markets or specialist sectors with creative ideas, seek quick scaling.
- Startups often search outside for venture capitalists, angel investors, or crowdsourcing sites due to high initial expenses and restricted income sources.
- Many entrepreneurs use technology to produce disruptive goods or services that drastically change the balance of power in the market.
- Depending on client comments and market needs, startups sometimes use agile approaches to hone their products.
- Although all startups are under the general heading of entrepreneurship, not all entrepreneurial activities qualify as startups. Many business owners may start small companies emphasizing sustainability and community impact instead of fast expansion.
- Innovation: Startups are constructed on fresh ideas that establish new markets or challenge accepted industry standards. New technology, methods, or business models are a few ways this creativity could appear.
- Scalability is one of the defining traits of startups, and it is their capacity for explosive expansion free from matching cost increases. Thanks to this scalability, startups can effectively reach more big markets and increase their activities.

- Startups are naturally oriented to reaching quick market penetration and growth. Their business models are meant to take advantage of early prospects and become somewhat well-known in their particular sectors.
- Many entrepreneurs use modern technologies driven by their need to improve their products and simplify processes. This technological emphasis gives them a competitive edge and helps them react fast to changing market conditions.
- Startups run in surroundings marked by great unpredictability and risk. From idea to market, one must negotiate difficulties like funding, creating workable products, and building consumer bases.

Startups' Contribution to the Economy

- Startups drive innovation, provide employment, and encourage competition, therefore playing an essential part in modern economies. One can find their influence in numerous spheres:
- Startups play a significant role in increasing employment. As they grow, they generate many employment possibilities and frequently use various skill sets across several departments.
- Startups increase economic activity and help to boost GDP by launching creative goods and services. Their capacity to upset existing sectors usually results in higher efficiency and output.
- Startups challenge conventional business processes, therefore stretching the bounds of invention. They frequently provide testing grounds for fresh ideas that might result in innovations in many fields.
- Compelling startups draw venture capitalists and angel investors who support their expansion and inspire more investment in the entrepreneurial environment.
- Many firms start with an eye toward overseas markets, improving their possible influence on the world economy. Their fast scalability can result in significant contributions outside of nearby areas.

Obstacles Startups Face

- Startups face many difficulties that could impede their success even with their significant influence:
- One of the toughest obstacles businesses face is finding finance. Many rely on venture money or angel contributions, which can be challenging

to find without a proven track record.

- Startups can join saturated markets where established companies rule. Against these incumbents, one must be strategically unique and employ good marketing.
- Growing firms must negotiate the complexity of increasing operations while preserving quality and customer happiness.
- Navigating legal and regulatory terrain can be extremely difficult for startups—especially those in highly regulated sectors like finance or healthcare.
- Attracting qualified staff can be challenging for startups vying with more prominent firms with more resources and stability.

Startups in India

Over the past ten years, India's startup scene has grown remarkably, rising to become among the biggest and most dynamic in the world. Following the United States and China, India is the third-largest startup hotspot worldwide as of April 2024, with over 128,000 identified businesses nationwide. This expansion can be ascribed to various reasons, including a young population, government programs, and rising investment interest.

Main Drivers of Expansion

Advantage of Demographic Change: Under 35 makes up a sizable fraction of India's population, offering a young workforce and a customer base receptive to fresh ideas and technology.

Initiatives like Startup India, which started in 2016, have been crucial in encouraging entrepreneurship using financing support, legislative changes, and incubator projects. The government has identified over 140,000 companies that have generated almost 1.55 million jobs.

India's software firms raised $11.3 billion in investment in 2024, a small rise from past years despite world economic difficulties. Venture capitalists and angel investors who are growingly interested in early-stage firms contribute to this funding scene.

Though fintech and e-commerce still rule, businesses in healthcare, agriculture, education, and sustainability are becoming more and more visible.

Difficulties Startups Face

Indian entrepreneurs have various difficulties even with the attractive environment:

Funding Restraints: Many businesses struggle to get sufficient money, particularly in the early years, even if financing has grown.

Obstacles in Regulations: For fledgling businesses, navigating complicated rules can be intimidating and affect their capacity for a successful scale.

Startups sometimes have to deal with established businesses that have more resources and brand awareness.

Attracting talented experts becomes more complex as competition for such talent grows.

Kashmirian startups: New prospects

- The entrepreneurial scene of Kashmir is starting to change as younger generations try to use local resources and solve socioeconomic issues by starting creative companies. Though historically well-known for its agriculture and handicaps, the area is seeing more tech-driven businesses today.
- Kashmir startups sometimes use traditional crafts like Pashmina shawls and papier-mâché art to produce distinctive goods appealing to local and international markets.
- Rich agricultural resources in the area offer chances for companies focused on horticulture, particularly with items like saffron and apples. For nearby farmers, creative supply chain solutions can help to increase earnings.
- Given Kashmir's reputation as a travel destination, firms providing digital platforms linking visitors with local guides and services or eco-tourism experiences could find success.

Problems unique to Kashmir

- The startup scene in Kashmir deals with unique difficulties:
- Political instability: Constant political events could make the surroundings of economic activities unclear.
- Infrastructure Restraints: Bad infrastructure might affect market access and logistics.
- Restricted Access to Funding: Entrepreneurs could find it challenging to get funding because of the region's apparent hazards.

Government Role

Governments all around have recently realized the need to encourage entrepreneurship and help startups as ways to increase economic development. Several projects have been started to foster entrepreneurial ecosystems, offering infrastructure support, mentoring programs, and financial aid. These initiatives are significant in areas where socioeconomic circumstances limit the conventional employment markets. Ultimately, startups and entrepreneurship are both essential parts of contemporary economies. They generate jobs, inspire creativity, and help to build general economic resilience. Knowing the subtleties of these ideas will benefit ambitious people. Through several government initiatives meant to offer financial support and training programs for aspirant entrepreneurs, attempts are being made to encourage entrepreneurship in Kashmir. Local talent is greatly nurtured, and a supportive ecosystem is created significantly by organizations like the Jammu and Kashmir Entrepreneurship Development Institute (JKEDI).

India's startup scene is flourishing and is driven by invention and government programs supporting entrepreneurship. Kashmir offers a special chance for aspiring business owners trying to use local resources while negotiating specific regional difficulties. Both ecosystems have great potential to support job creation and economic development in their particular settings as they keep changing.

Startups are a dynamic force in the economy distinguished by creativity, scalability, and an emphasis on solving real-world problems with technologically driven solutions. Their influence goes beyond simple employment; they stimulate innovation in many fields and economic development. Although there are many difficulties, the possible benefits of effective startup businesses make them a necessary part of modern economic environments since they promote entrepreneurship that propels development and transformation. In a growing competitive setting, entrepreneurs maximize their chances for success by more precisely navigating their paths.

II

Startup Journey: From Idea to Execution

Beginning a business is like sowing a seed. The concept is the seed; with the correct care—that comes from strategy, tools, and execution—it develops into a profitable business. From idea to the critical phases of validation, planning, and execution, this chapter offers a necessary road map for turning a vision into reality.

1. Idea and brainstorming

Every startup starts its road from an idea. Your idea is the pillar of your entrepreneurial journey, whether it results from a problem you have faced, a passion you wish to follow, or a market possibility you have found. Success depends on spotting a problem and knowing how your solution may specifically solve it, add value, and satisfy market needs.

The best startup concepts address specific issues since they are the core.

- In your neighbourhood or target market, what obstacles must individuals overcome?
- Exist any areas where current systems could be strengthened?
- How might one make value additions to people's lives?

These fundamental questions help one grasp the actual wants your company could handle. Emphasising problem-solving guarantees that your business will survive and flourish by providing a solution that appeals to consumers.

Long-term sustainability, which depends on matching your interests and abilities with industry needs. Your enthusiasm will be the engine keeping you motivated during the ups and downs of business. Concurrent with this is the need to know market demand to guarantee that your company idea is profitable and capable of running. Should your concept be based on market need and passion, you are likelier to stay to it even under challenging circumstances. This alignment drives you and increases your chances of creating a company people desire and are ready to pay for.

Idea refinement and brainstorming:

List all possible ideas, regardless of their seeming oddity.

Talk about them to get several points of view with mentors, friends, or possible clients. Interacting with people from all backgrounds and points of view will help you to find weaknesses or missed possibilities in your ideas. They might probe gently or offer observations you hadn't thought of.

Limit your attention to a viable, scalable concept consistent with your long-term objectives. After you have an idea list, assess them against these standards. A solid company idea is realistic and scalable—capable of increasing over time and, if necessary, reaching a bigger market. It should also always fit your personal and professional objectives to be relevant and fulfilling.

Remember that this approach is iterative even as you hone your concept. Before deciding on a notion that seems correct, you might go through multiple rounds of review and modification. Especially when you compile additional data and comments, be honest about changing and pivoting if needed. The aim is to arrive at an idea that is creative but also sensible and durable.

Valuating your idea comes next once you have a polished and clear one. This implies challenging your presumptions and compiling actual data to guarantee your good or service has market demand. Building a strong startup depends on validation—interacting with possible consumers to learn their requirements and preferences.

2. Verifying the Viability of Your Idea (Validation)

Valuation of your idea is vital before devoting major work and money. Validation guarantees that your good or service will appeal to your target market and be successful on the shelves. This phase is about proving that you can handle the issues your possible clients run against and that there is an actual demand for your offer. You must compile information, challenge presumptions, and iterate depending on actual comments to hone your idea.

Industry Research:

Engage directly with your target audience to grasp their wants, preferences, and pain areas using surveys and conversations with possible consumers. Find out from open-ended questions how they would use your good or service and what they would be ready to pay for it. This stage enables you to compile qualitative information to support or contradict your first presumptions.

Examine related goods or services on the market to find gaps and prospects. Where are they lacking, and at what level do they excel? This study can find underserved niches or unmet demands your company could be able to satisfy. It also helps you arrange your offering to distinguish itself from the competitors.

Investigate industry trends and needs using online tools; track customer behaviour through digital platforms and analytics. Industry studies, SEMrush, and Google Trends, among other tools, can offer insightful analysis of what is currently in demand and which markets can show future development.

Prototyping

Create a simple version of your good or service or a minimal viable product (MVP), a condensed form with the most essential aspects. It is meant to evaluate your idea in the market with a low initial outlay. This phase lets you compile user comments and assess the feasibility of your concept before deciding on a significant release.

Test the MVP with a small group of users to acquire comments:

Ask a focused population that fits your ideal clientele comments. See how they would enhance the product, what they enjoy or dislike, and how they engage with it. This direct contact can offer priceless information on what has to be changed and how your product satisfies consumer expectations.

Iterate depending on insights to enhance your offering; change your MVP in response to comments. This can involve adjusting the user interface, honing functionality, or altering your value proposition. Perfecting your product to satisfy consumers' wants depends on the iterative process.

Testing business models:

- Establish your cost structure and income sources: Know how your company will turn a profit and what running expenses would demand. This covers several income sources, such as sales, subscriptions, advertising, or alliances. Calculate your initial and continuing expenses—production, distribution, marketing, staffing, etc.

- Determine possible obstacles to scaling your company: Consider what could stop it from expanding. Do supply chains, regulations, or market entry hurdles call for addressing? Early identification of these difficulties helps you create action plans to go beyond them.

- Get early comments from mentors, advisers, or industry professionals who might offer a reality check on your company plan. They can provide direction on scalability, market entrance, and price policies. Their knowledge will enable you to improve your company model and become more assertive and flexible in demanding conditions.

Developing a strong business plan:

Your startup's blueprint comes from a business plan. It details your vision, approach, and road plan for execution. Not only does a thorough plan direct your activities, but it also draws partners and investors. Clearly defining your business idea, getting money, and persuading stakeholders of your value proposition depends on a well-considered business plan.

Essential elements of a business plan are

- **Executive Summary**: Your company idea and objectives are succinctly summed up here. It should contain the unique value proposition, the mission statement, and the company's goals. The first part of the corporate plan, the executive summary, should be brief yet intense enough to grab the reader's attention.

- **Market Analysis**: Share your target market and rivals in great detail. Demographic information, customer behaviour, and trends should all fall into this category. It should also include a SWOT analysis—strengths, weaknesses, opportunities, threats—to assist you in determining your competitive posture and possible obstacles.

- **Describe your good or service** and how it addresses a market need or problem. This part should go into great length on the qualities and advantages of your good or service and how it stands out from competitors.

- Specify how you will draw in and keep consumers in terms of marketing and sales strategy. List your sales techniques, customer acquisition plans, and marketing outlets. Online marketing, alliances, direct sales, or other strategies meant to reach your target market could all fit here.

-

Financial Projections: Add approximated profit margins, costs, and income. This part should present a clear financial picture of your company, including beginning expenses, break-even points, and anticipated profitability over time. One should be realistic and present facts that back up their financial presumptions.

The second is like the Business Model Canvas, which will help you to lay out your company concept graphically. This tool addresses essential elements like these to enable you to conceptualise and validate your company idea:

- **Value proposition**: What worth does your company offer to the client? How might it improve their lives or help them solve their problems?
- **Customer segments:** Who are your target clients? Their demographics, actions, and requirements:
- **Important resources and activities**: What main ones does your company require to run? What human, financial, and technological resources do you need?
- **Cost structure and income sources**: How will you create income? Delivery of your good or service comes with expenses.

Clearly defining objectives:

- Clearly state quantifiable goals that are in line with your company strategy.
- Objectives should be SMART—specific, measurable, achievable, relevant, and time-bound.
- Reaching a specified number of consumers, obtaining money, introducing a new product, or turning a profit within a given period could all fall under the examples here.
- Divide your ambitions into reasonable steps to create both long-term visions and short-term benchmarks.
- Short-term goals include attaining a specific sales target, testing a fresh marketing plan, or gathering first client comments.
- Long-term goals could call for growing the company worldwide, introducing fresh products, or entering new markets.
- While accomplishing little victories along the road, setting both goals offers a clear road forward and keeps you orientated on the big picture.

3. Execution: Turning Ideas into Reality

Ideas are turned into concrete outcomes via execution. It includes assembling your staff, acquiring capital, and starting your company. This is the stage of realising your vision using efficient implementation of ideas. It's about organising your resources, assembling a team, getting money, and finally releasing your good or service onto the market. Success at this level calls for precise coordination, open communication, and unrelenting attention to produce outcomes.

Selecting the Correct Team:

- Decide which primary responsibilities your startup needs: Find the ones to run it properly. Your business model will determine if this covers positions including marketing, operations, finance, product development, customer service, and more. Every position should complement your long-term goal and help your company to be core competent.
- Look for team members whose experience closes holes in your skill set; their abilities complement yours and fit your vision. A well-rounded team is one in which every member offers a strength. This variation will help your company to innovate more freely and negotiate obstacles more successfully.
- Encourage a culture of teamwork and lifelong learning; the success of a startup depends on a good team dynamic. Promote honest communication, mutual respect, and a readiness to grow personally from one another. More incredible innovation and problem-solving can result from a cooperative culture whereby team members feel supported and empowered to provide their finest ideas.

Funding Your Business:

- Investigate numerous funding sources; your startup can be financed from many directions. Start with your savings, kin and friends help. Though they have return responsibilities, bank loans might offer another source of money. If you are seeking outside investors capable of providing finance and strategic direction, venture capital is possible. Government grants and programs especially meant to help startups also provide non-dilutive financing should you meet particular requirements.

- Take advantage of government funds or programs designed for startups; many areas have grants and initiatives meant to boost local businesses. These can be a great source of early-stage money and occasionally include other resources, such as business development help and mentoring.
- Whether you are looking for angel investors, venture capitalists, or another kind of finance, your pitch to investors needs to succinctly convey your company's value proposition, your development plan, and how you intend to spend the money. A skillfully written pitch should explain why investors should believe in your concept and the possible return on investment. A strong pitch depends mostly on practice, clarity, and confidence.

Start Your Product or Service:

Using digital marketing techniques, social media, news releases, local events, and networking, create awareness about your launch and draw early adopters. Establish a community around your good or service on Facebook, Instagram, Twitter, and LinkedIn sites. Speak with journalists, influencers, and possible consumers to help to spread the word.

- Provide first-time buyers discounts or specials to draw in business; first-time clients are vital for your company's credibility and momentum development. To inspire customers to test your good or service, consider running early bird specials, buy-one-get-one offers, or limited-time discounts. Depending on user answers, early sales, feedback collecting, and improved offerings can all come from this.
- Always get comments and make changes following the launch; the launch marks only the start. Closely review client comments to learn what performs and what doesn't. Based on these comments, change your good or service to raise user retention and satisfaction. The startup process is mostly iterative; thus, being sensitive to client needs can help you stand out from rivals and build loyalty among them.
- Implementing a company plan calls for both strategic thinking and tactical execution in concert. You can realise your entrepreneurial goal by assembling the appropriate team, ensuring enough capital, and introducing your product under a well-coordinated strategy. This stage is about making sure your company picks momentum and creates conditions for continuous expansion, not only about starting.

The function of technology in execution

Technology may greatly simplify your startup's running processes and enhance client experience. Using the correct tools and platforms may improve the efficiency of your procedures, raise output, and enable better client involvement. Whether your startup is in project management, marketing, sales, e-commerce, or another field, technology can be important in determining its success.

Project handling:

- Task management tools such as Trello or Asana let you set deadlines, arrange chores and monitor progress, keeping every team member in line. They help to keep production high by providing a graphic means of project management, team member collaboration, and task prioritising, thereby optimising processes.
- Use these instruments to distribute work, create due dates, and keep track of project milestones. This helps you control your workload and lets you quickly modify strategies in reaction to evolving conditions.

Marketing:

- Make advantage of social media channels to interact with possible consumers on Facebook, Instagram, Twitter, and LinkedIn. Sharing material, developing a brand, and interacting with your audience can all be accomplished on social media. Reaching the correct people with your message will depend on using analytics and focused marketing.
- Email marketing and SEO: Mailchimp or HubSpot can assist you in categorising your audience, tracking open rates and conversions, and automating email campaigns. Google Analytics and SEMrush, among other SEO tools, let you track website traffic, find keywords, and edit material to raise search engine results.
- Content marketing: Use technology to create, oversee, and disseminate material throughout several outlets. Value can be shared, and possible clients can be drawn in using blogs, videos, infographics, and podcasts. Post scheduling, email list management, and engagement tracking capabilities of automation tools help.

Customer Relationship Management and Sales:

- Manage customer relationships with Salesforce or HubSpot; CRM solutions are vital for recording client contacts, lead management, and prospect development. They enable you to follow up on questions, track client satisfaction, and seal deals by keeping all customer data in one location.
- In analytics and reporting, leverage CRM data to understand consumer behaviour, preferences, and sales performance. This knowledge can direct your sales plan and support wise decision-making.

E-commerce

- Create an online store with Shopify or WooCommerce; these e-commerce systems simplify inventory management, payment processing, order tracking, and building of an online store. They provide plugins, templates, and interfaces that enable rapid and effective company scale.
- Ensure your e-commerce store is mobile-friendly and that the purchasing process flows naturally and clearly. Rapid growth in mobile commerce means that a good mobile experience can considerably raise consumer happiness and sales.

Learning from Errors and Changing

- Every strategy will not function exactly. Hence, mistakes are unavoidable on the entrepreneurial path. Most important is your capacity for learning and adaptation. An excellent quality of successful businesspeople is their capacity to recover from failures, examine errors, and improve tactics.
- Aggressively solicit helpful critique from clients, team members, mentors, and advisers. Even negative comments offer insightful analysis that will let you know what works and what doesn't. Make changes and modify your business plan using this input.

Analysing mistakes

Determine what went wrong and how to prevent future errors: Examine failures and setbacks closely to find the underlying reasons. Was it a misjudged marketing plan, a matter of market fit, or a product issue? Finding these problems enables you to prevent repeating the same mistakes and make wise judgements going forward.

Maintain resilience.

Develop an attitude of tenacity and hope; ups and downs abound on the road to entrepreneurship. Crucially, developing resilience and keeping upbeat in the face of hardship. Keep dedicated to your vision and be ready to veer when needed. Your success will finally be driven by tenacity and a readiness to grow from mistakes.

There are countless chances, challenges, and excitement on the startup road. Starting with a well-defined idea, validating it, carefully planning, and executing with clarity will help you build a strong company using a disciplined strategy. Entrepreneurship is a dynamic activity that calls for both ongoing education and adaptation. Stay true to your goal, keep open to comments, and enthusiastically welcome the road as you start your trek.

III

Startup Ecosystem: Resources and Networks

The foundation of entrepreneurial success is a vibrant start-up ecosystem providing tools, support, and direction at every path level. Overcoming obstacles and developing their businesses depends on budding Kashmiri entrepreneurs knowing and using the resources. With an eye towards accelerators, incubators, and finance, this part explores the key elements of the start-up ecosystem.

1. Role of accelerators, incubators, and funding.

Accelerators: Encouraging Development

Designed to fast-track the growth of entrepreneurs, accelerators provide mentoring, funding, and networking chances within a set period. They are helpful for businesses regarding idea development, investor contact, and market launch of their products.

Mentorship and Structured Learning:

- Accelerators offer a set course catered to start-up requirements. Workshops, seminars, and one-on-one mentoring meetings emphasise honing company ideas, polishing pitches, and tackling particular pain issues.
- Participating in accelerator programs could enable Kashmiri businesses to meet industry professionals who know how to negotiate sociopolitical issues that are particular to their area.

Funding and investor accessibility:

Many accelerators provide introductions to venture capitalists and angel investors and provide seed money as part of their offerings. This access can alter everything for start-ups seeking financial backing to expand their activities.

Networks

One can find great value in the contacts formed during an accelerator program. Relationships with other start-ups, business alliances, and networks build a community that encourages development and creativity.

Incubators: Developing Concepts into Reality

Although incubators are meant to assist entrepreneurs in developing their basic ideas into profitable companies, accelerators concentrate on scaling start-ups. In less time-bound surroundings, they offer resources, infrastructure, and mentoring.

Digital and Physical Resources:

Shared workspaces, tool and technology access, and support services, including legal and administrative help, abound at incubators. For Kashmirian companies, these tools can help to close the disparity produced by inadequate local infrastructure.

Individualised Assistance

Often working closely with entrepreneurs, incubators provide individualised direction. They enable creators to test prototypes, hone their value proposition, and create go-to-market plans catered to local dynamics.

Support Localised Solutions:

While guaranteeing scalability for larger markets, incubators in Kashmir might inspire entrepreneurs to develop solutions addressing local challenges, including using technology for agriculture, tourism, or handicrafts.

Money: Igniting the Start-up Engine

One of the most challenging obstacles entrepreneurs must overcome is access to cash; hence, success depends on finding the correct kind of financing at the right moment. Entrepreneurs have to investigate several funding sources and know their consequences.

Bootstrapping:

Many business owners use their money or look to family and friends for financial help. Although this method gives more control, scalability is often limited.

For instance, a Kashmiri craftsperson starting an online store can start with personal money before looking for outside investment for marketing and growth.

Government Awards and Subsidies:

Governments sometimes provide grants, subsidies, and low-interest loans to help businesses, particularly in underdeveloped areas. Programs catered to Kashmir's socioeconomic situation can assist in closing financing gaps and inspire creativity.

Venture bankers and angel investors:

While venture capitalists oversee money put in high-growth firms, angel investors offer capital in return for stock or convertible debt. For companies who have confirmed their market potential, these sources are perfect for scaling.

Platforms for crowding funding:

Entrepreneurs can raise money from many backers via crowdsourcing sites like Kickstarter, Indiegogo, or localised counterparts. This strategy offers money and confirms the demand for the good in the market.

Microloans and Bank Loans:

Start-ups with strong creditworthiness and business plans can find consistent financing from banks and microfinance organisations. Microfinance programs catering to small enterprises might be helpful for local businesspeople in Kashmir.

Using Networks for Success

Beyond set initiatives and limited funds, your development depends significantly on the relationships you create inside the start-up. Networking facilitates peer learning, mentoring searches, and cooperative project exploration.

Local and worldwide connections:

Connecting with local business leaders, diaspora networks, and worldwide communities helps Kashmir's entrepreneurs. Such ties create portals to information, new markets, and alliances.

Attendance of Start-up Events:

Participating in hackathons, pitch contests, and start-up expos will enable founders to present their ideas, draw in funding, and learn about market trends.

Consolidating Professional Groups:

Participating in groups like trade associations, chambers of business, or online communities helps companies to keep current, share ideas, and get help as needed.

Though still under development, Kashmir's start-up environment has an excellent capacity to foster entrepreneurship. Entrepreneurs can break through obstacles, polish their ideas, and grow their companies using accelerators, incubators, and financing possibilities. More significantly, creating strong networks and interacting with the ecosystem guarantees that start-ups survive and flourish in a constantly shifting environment. Success comes from using these tools, adjusting to local and worldwide problems, and not wavering in the search for creativity.

2. Collaboration and Networking Possibilities

Any active entrepreneurial environment is primarily dependent on networking and teamwork. Establishing relationships and creating alliances can help Kashmir's businesses access vital resources, inspire creativity, and open doors to new markets. Entrepreneurs ' active engagement with peers, mentors, and industry stakeholders dramatically increases their chances of success. This section looks at the value of networking and teamwork and provides practical advice on best using these opportunities.

Networking's Worth

Networking is about developing deep relationships that enhance your entrepreneurial path, not attending events or gathering business cards. Strong networks give access to knowledge, mentoring, tools, and possibilities that might otherwise stay beyond grasp.

Broadening Your Knowledge Base:

Speaking with seasoned business owners and industry professionals may offer priceless insights on overcoming obstacles, spotting trends, and making wise decisions.

For instance, a Kashmir tourism firm might pick creative customer interaction techniques from speaking with a worldwide eco-tourism guru.

Creating Credibility:

Developing ties with well-known players in the start-up scene will help you build Credibility and draw partners or funding. Often acting as endorsements, trusted relationships help to inspire stakeholders' confidence.

Expanding New Markets:

Networking with people from different sectors or areas might result in alliances to increase your clientele or investigate unserved markets.

Cooperation: Strength in Consensus

Networking is closely related to cooperation since it helps start-ups to pool resources, exchange expertise, and co-create solutions. For Kashmirian entrepreneurs, group initiatives can be beneficial in tackling local problems and operations growth.

Innovation and Co-Creation:

Combining complementary knowledge with other start-ups or established companies can stimulate innovation.

For instance, a tech firm might work with a classic handicraft company to create an online platform, bringing local artists to a worldwide audience.

Resource Sharing:

Start-ups can exchange tools, physical space, or knowledge via means of collaboration, therefore lowering costs and improving productivity. Two best examples of this advantage are shared tools and co-working environments.

Branding and joint marketing:

Cooperative marketing initiatives, including collaborative events or cross-promotion, can increase visibility and reach for all those engaged.

Techniques for Superior Networking and Teamwork

Though the advantages are apparent, networking and teamwork require careful preparation and active involvement. Entrepreneurs should approach these events with well-defined goals and a ready desire to participate.

Events and forums:

Industry expos, local and international start-up events, and pitch contests. Such events allow interaction with possible consumers, partners, and investors.

For instance, a start-up conference in Kashmir may be a central gathering for businesspeople to present ideas and form relations with other firms.

Making use of digital channels:

Online sites, including LinkedIn, AngelList, and industry-specific forums, present chances and opportunities with mentors, investors, and partners. All entrepreneurs can join specialised groups, engage in conversations, and create online relationships, resulting in actual possibilities.

Interacting with nearby communities:

Working with government agencies, non-profits, or local businesses can enable entrepreneurs to match their needs with available resources for expansion.

For instance, a firm with a sustainability concentration might collaborate with nearby environmental organisations to advance green living.

Combining Accelerators and Incubators:

These initiatives give organised settings for cooperation and networking. They frequently feature events meant for entrepreneurs to network with business executives and each other, hence generating alliances and synergy.

Establishing strategic alliances:

Find companies with complementary capabilities and shared objectives, then create official alliances to co-develop goods or services, distribute networks, or cooperatively handle market difficulties.

Changing to a contributor:

Networking is about giving, not only about taking. Share your knowledge, help others, and become a valued part of the ecology—usually, a reputation for being helpful results in reciprocal opportunities.

Managing Difficulties in Networking

Though significant, networking and teamwork present particular difficulties, particularly in Kashmir, where the start-up scene is still developing. Entrepreneurs have to be ready to handle these difficulties aggressively.

Participating in virtual communities and attending regional or national events can help offset restricted access to known start-up networks.

Establishing Confidence:

Effective teams depend on trust being established. Lasting relationships start with open communication, well-defined roles, and mutual respect.

Juggling Efforts

Networking may take time. Entrepreneurs must combine their attention on their primary business operations with developing relationships.

A successful start-up depends on networking and teamwork; these are not optional elements. These initiatives can help Kashmiri entrepreneurs close resource gaps, encourage creativity, and give the support required to meet particular geographical difficulties. Entrepreneurs can turn their ideas into successful businesses by actively participating in the start-up environment, using local and worldwide networks, and welcoming teamwork. In business, success primarily depends on the strength of deep ties and shared goals; it is hardly a solitary path.

3. Leveraging technology and digital tools.

Technology is not just a luxury but also a need for start-ups trying to survive and grow in the fast-changing corporate scene of today. Using digital tools and technologies allows Kashmiri businesses to overcome political, logistical, geographical and administrative obstacles. Whether it's improving consumer involvement, simplifying processes, or broadening market reach, judicious use of technology may be revolutionary.

Changing Activities Using Technology

Technology lets firms run effectively with few resources by automating complex tasks.

Tools of Project Management:

Among other tools, Monday.com, Asana, and Trello assist with task distribution, deadline tracking, and team coordination. These systems centralise project management so business owners can concentrate on high-priority tasks and maintain consistency throughout all operations.

Finance and Accounting Management:

Platforms, including QuickBooks, Zoho Books, and Xero, help track costs, manage budgets, and create financial reports, guaranteeing a professional and accurate approach to financial planning.

Supply chain and inventory management:

Retail, handcraft, or agricultural start-ups can use TradeGecko or Odoo to control inventory, simplify supply chains, and guarantee on-time delivery.

Improving Client Engagement

Thanks to technology, start-ups now have creative means to interact with clients, create relationships, and provide value.

Marketing Social Media:

Start-ups can now access a more extensive audience thanks to sites including Facebook, Instagram, and Twitter. Targeting ad campaigns, sharing interesting material, and engaging followers will help companies raise consumer loyalty and brand exposure.

E-mail marketing:

Mailchimp or Constant Contact tools let companies keep a consistent and professional communication channel by sending personalised messages, promotions, and updates to possible and current clients.

CRM—customer relationship management:

Start-ups track customer interactions, manage leads, and analyse customer behaviour using CRMs such as HubSpot, Salesforce, or Zoho CRM, thus improving sales and service tactics.

Increasing Market Share

Sustained development for Kashmir's start-ups depends on them surpassing local markets. Technology provides means for worldwide development and close distances.

E-commerce systems:

By enabling companies to sell goods online, sites like Shopify, WooCommerce, or Amazon help them reach consumers all over. Local artists, for instance, can present Kashmiri handcrafted goods to a global market using these methods.

Digital payments:

PayPal, Stripe, or Razorpay's safe and easy payment gateways help firms provide flawless transactions, increasing client confidence and happiness.

Remote work and Internet collaboration:

Start-ups can use Zoom, Slack, or Google Workspace tools to collaborate with teams, customers, and partners, thereby promoting innovation and efficiency despite physical distances.

Data-Driven Decision Making

Thanks to data analytics instruments, start-ups can make better decisions by knowing market trends, consumer preferences, and performance criteria.

Tracking website traffic, user behaviour, and conversion rates, platforms like Google Analytics offer insightful information to improve user experience and hone marketing plans.

Business intelligence instruments:

Tools such as Tableau or Power BI turn raw data into valuable insights, enabling businesses to identify prospects and reduce risks.

Social Listening Tools:

Start-ups staying ahead of trends and tackling issues early on can track internet references, customer reviews, and market sentiment using technologies like Hootsuite or Sprout Social.

Overcoming Local Obstacles with Technology

The particular socioeconomic setting of Kashmir brings difficulties, but technology provides customised answers.

E-Learning and Instruction:

Without having to leave the area, sites like Udemy, Coursera, or LinkedIn Learning let businesses upskill their staff and themselves.

Advancements in Telecommunication:

Tools for virtual collaboration, messaging, and video conferences enable us to overcome connectivity issues, guaranteeing business continuity even in trying conditions.

Localised Solutions:

Start-ups can use technologies for local requirements, such as agritech solutions for nearby farms or mobile banking for places with inadequate banking facilities. For Kashmirian start-ups, success depends primarily on strategic technological adoption. Entrepreneurs can overcome regional constraints and set their businesses for long-term development using digital tools for operations, consumer involvement, and market expansion. Technology levels the playing field and enables companies to compete worldwide, fostering creativity and fortitude against adversity.

The start-up scene of Kashmir is developing into a dynamic network of resources, chances, and difficulties. Although traditional sectors such as tourism, handicrafts, and agriculture provide the backbone of the economy, a new wave of innovation propelled by accelerators, incubators, and digital technologies is developing. Understanding and using these tools is essential for the success of would-be business owners.

Accelerators and incubators are extensively developing Kashmir's entrepreneurial ability. Helping businesses negotiate the early phases of business development, these sites offer mentoring, office space, and finance access. Though fewer such initiatives exist in Kashmir than in other cities, the existing ones have a significant influence. Local incubators, for instance, promote agri-tech, eco-tourism, and e-commerce projects by concentrating on closing the gap between traditional sectors and current business practices.

One of the primary difficulties Kashmiri entrepreneurs face still is getting money. Because of strict criteria, traditional finance sources, including bank loans, are sometimes unreachable; venture capital participation is rare. To offset this, entrepreneurs are looking at other funding sources, including government-sponsored programs and crowdsourcing. Offering grants, subsidies, and tax advantages, programs like Jammu & Kashmir's Start-up Policy and Start-up India initiative are opening routes for financial support. Another vital component of creating a viable firm is networking. In Kashmir, where official networking activities are rare, unofficial networks and community-based cooperation often fill in. Using social media channels, entrepreneurs are reaching out to mentors, peers, and possible investors more and more. As colleges and universities start to include entrepreneurship in their courses and encourage innovation through hackathons and contests, networking possibilities also result from partnerships between academia and industry.

Working together is starting to define the environment. Though relatively new to the area, co-working spaces are becoming increasingly popular as centres where businesspeople from many backgrounds may trade resources and ideas. Particularly in an area where access to official business support systems is restricted, these venues promote knowledge-sharing and a feeling of community, therefore fostering vital skills.

Fostering Innovation and Growth: National Buyer-Seller Meet at SKICC Highlights Promising Startups from the Kashmir Valley

For start-ups in Kashmir, technology is a game-changer since it provides tools and platforms to solve many of the fundamental problems of the area. Though uneven, companies are accessing markets well beyond local limits as cell phones and internet access become increasingly ubiquitous. From customer relationship management (CRM) to marketing and analytics, digital solutions simplify processes, including inventory control. While using social media for branding and customer interaction, entrepreneurs build online shopfronts on sites like Shopify and WooCommerce.
Technology's application also reaches knowledge gathering and networking. Entrepreneurs can network with business experts and learn from worldwide best practices by means of sites like LinkedIn and start-ups'

dedicated forums. Gradually adopting data-driven decision-making, local businesses are leveraging analytics to grasp market trends and improve their products.

Even with these developments, social and cultural conventions nevertheless provide ongoing difficulties. Stable government employment often takes the front stage in traditional expectations, which fosters a risk-averse attitude by excluding entrepreneurial activities. Women entrepreneurs must also contend with social limitations and restricted resources. Dealing with these problems requires a multi-pronged strategy combining awareness campaigns, legislative changes, and mentoring programs to strengthen underprivileged populations.

In essence, the start-up scene in Kashmir is at a turning point. The area has excellent potential driven by its rich resources and young vitality, despite its unique difficulties. Entrepreneurs can create strong companies that support the socioeconomic change in the area by using digital tools, financial sources, and accelerators. The drivers behind this change will be cooperation, flexibility, and relentless innovation commitment.

IV

Kashmir: A Land of Untapped Potential

Often praised for its stunning scenery and rich cultural legacy, Kashmir is also a nation full of unrealised economic possibilities. Although the area's natural beauty and traditional crafts have won praise, its entrepreneurial potential is still significantly underdeveloped. Those with a strong awareness of the socio-economic complexities of the area and the vision to use its particular advantages have transforming chances for creativity, expansion, and progress.

1. Unique challenges and opportunities for entrepreneurs in Kashmir.

Kashmiri entrepreneurship is a complex and multifarious endeavour with both opportunities and difficulties. The area boasts many natural resources, a tradition of expert artistry, and a young, aspirational populace ready to forge new directions. These elements lay a strong basis for business activities. But the road is full of challenges like poor infrastructure, limited market access, and the uncertainty brought on by political unrest. Notwithstanding these obstacles, or maybe because of them, Kashmir offers a unique canvas for innovative and tenacious businesses to leave their mark.

The **traditional businesses** of the area are among its most important assets since they have been fundamental to its economy for ages. The three pillars defining Kashmir's cultural identity are handcrafts, horticulture, and tourism; they also provide excellent opportunities for innovation and modernisation. For instance, artists who create beautiful walnut wood carvings, complex papier-mâché objects, and stunning **Pashmina shawls** have skills unparalleled anywhere. However, the absence of contemporary marketing channels and intermediaries sometimes means these artists get little compensation for their efforts. Entrepreneurs can close this gap by bringing worldwide e-commerce sites devoted to handcrafted goods. By allowing artisans to reach global markets straight-forward, these platforms can help to ensure fair pay and preserve the legacy connected with their works. Furthermore, branding techniques stressing the sustainability and authenticity of these products might open premium markets, especially in nations where ethical consumerism is becoming more and more common.

Kashmiri Carpet-Source: Elrex Trading

Even **horticulture** has excellent potential. Already a significant participant in these markets, Kashmir is well-known for its walnuts, saffron, and premium apples. Meanwhile, its full potential is hampered by post-harvest losses, supply chain inefficiencies, and changing market access. Here, AgriTech and agricultural startups can transform quite a lot. These businesses may boost output and guarantee that Kashmir's produce reaches worldwide markets in ideal condition by bringing technologies, including artificial intelligence for crop monitoring, blockchain for ensuring quality and traceability, and cold storage options. By enabling farmers to command better prices for their goods, farm-to-market systems that link producers straight with consumers might help to reduce inefficiencies further.

Often referred to as the backbone of Kashmir's economy, **tourism** presents yet unrivalled chances for entrepreneurial creativity. Although the area's natural beauty draws tourists in large numbers, speciality travel experiences, including eco-tourism, adventure tourism, and cultural tourism, are in increasing demand. Emphasising sustainability and authenticity, entrepreneurs can create original vacation plans that fit these developing tastes. For a discriminating audience looking for significant travel experiences, trekking trips in the Himalayas, immersive village stays, or gourmet excursions exploring the rich gastronomic traditions can draw in. Digital channels that let visitors schedule such encounters quickly and safely can also help the sector.

Regency Hotel in Pahalgam, Kashmir

Although conventional sectors offer a solid basis, the real future of entrepreneurship in Kashmir lies in developing industries that meet essential requirements and welcome technology developments. The digital revolution has provided fresh opportunities for companies to run free from geographical limitations. Startups concentrated on technologically enabled solutions are already starting to show their presence. Kashmir boasts vast tech entrepreneurial potential from software creation to **IT services to app-based solutions**. A digital marketplace for local crafts, a mobile app letting users schedule environmentally friendly journeys, or an artificial intelligence-based platform for agricultural advice services can all help to tackle actual problems while generating economic value.

Two sectors vital to the welfare and development of any area, education and healthcare, also have unrealised potential in Kashmir. The area's youth might lack access to chances for skill development and high-quality education. Younger generations can be equipped with the tools to participate in the global economy using online learning platforms, vocational training centres, and skill development programs. Likewise, the healthcare industry—which suffers from restricted access to specialised services—can profit much from telemedicine businesses. Platforms that link clinicians in far-off locations with patients or offer digital health monitoring tools help close critical healthcare system gaps.

Though great promise exists, it is impossible to ignore the difficulties of Kashmiri business. Entrepreneurs have to negotiate with resilience and adaptable reality of socio-political uncertainty, regular interruptions, and infrastructure shortcomings. These very difficulties, nevertheless, can offer chances for creative ideas. For example, while logistics companies can develop innovative ways to handle supply chain interruptions, decentralised energy solutions like solar microgrids can help to solve power shortages. Those who handle these challenges with creativity and tenacity can make them competitive advantages.

The scene of entrepreneurship in Kashmir is just a turning point. The area might become a centre of creative and sustainable business with the correct mix of strategic insight, technical innovation, and classic strengths. Rising to the occasion, entrepreneurs not only create profitable businesses but also help to further more general objectives such as social resilience, cultural preservation, and economic empowerment. Driven by the spirit of invention and the will to achieve, Kashmir's tale is one of promise—a territory with all the tools to become a dynamic entrepreneurial ecosystem.

2. Understanding the socio-economic landscape.

Entrepreneurs hoping to start profitable businesses in Kashmir must first understand the socio-economic scene of the area. Historically, Kashmir's economy has been rural, with a significant focus on horticulture as a primary engine of economic growth. Apple farming, saffron growing, and walnut production are celebrated for their quality and demand. However, inefficiencies in the supply chain, inadequate access to contemporary technologies, and difficulties scaling production have kept these sectors from realising their best possibilities. Those who can include innovation in these conventional sectors—using blockchain for supply chain transparency or artificial intelligence for crop management—have the chance to transform these sectors.

Unemployment is a significant problem, especially for the educated young. Though this is starting to change, the inclination for steady government employment has always dictated how one thinks. Young people's growing enthusiasm for business shows their need for creativity and independence. Still, significant obstacles limit their aspirations. Common challenges are limited access to mentoring programs, a dearth of strong funding sources, and underdeveloped entrepreneurial infrastructure. Programs emphasising capacity building—such as seminars, incubators, and government-supported startup projects—may act as accelerators for releasing the entrepreneurial potential of the area.

Socio-political questions still add another level of complexity to the entrepreneurial terrain. The area has seen disturbances that can compromise company continuity, market access, and supply chains. Entrepreneurs must address these obstacles with resilience and adaptation, guaranteeing contingency preparations and operational flexibility. Although these ambiguities can be intimidating, they also present chances for companies who supply stability-oriented solutions. For example, logistics businesses that can overcome disruptions or digital markets by removing physical dependencies can succeed in such surroundings.

Notwithstanding these difficulties, Kashmir's unique socio-economic profile also offers different chances. Among the great treasures of the area are its natural riches, artistic creations, and rich cultural legacy. Entrepreneurs who match their projects with local capabilities and worldwide market needs can release steady development. For example, presenting Kashmiri art on digital media or creating luxury organic food goods with obvious provenance stories will draw attention from all around.

Recognising and meeting local populations' needs and ambitions also helps one understand the socio-economic context. Constructing businesses that create jobs, raise living conditions, and empower underprivileged populations can create a chain reaction of good changes. Entrepreneurs who see their companies as tools of social influence and profit-driven entities can help promote long-term sustainability and goodwill. Startups in Kashmir can overcome obstacles and help the area become a dynamic centre of innovation and opportunity by adopting a comprehensive awareness of the socio-economic scene.

3. The importance of cultural and geographical factors.

Entrepreneurs hoping to start profitable businesses in Kashmir must first understand the socio-economic scene of the area. Historically, Kashmir's economy has been rural, with a significant focus on horticulture as a primary engine of economic growth. Apple farming, saffron growing, and walnut production are celebrated for their quality and demand. However, inefficiencies in the supply chain, inadequate access to contemporary technologies, and difficulties scaling production have kept these sectors from realising their best possibilities. Those who can include innovation in these conventional sectors—using blockchain for supply chain transparency or artificial intelligence for crop management—have the chance to transform these sectors.

Unemployment is a significant problem, especially for the educated young in the area. Though this is starting to change, the inclination for steady government employment has always dictated how one thinks. Young people's growing enthusiasm for business shows their need for creativity and independence. Still, major obstacles limit their aspirations. Common challenges are limited access to mentoring programs, a dearth of strong funding sources, and underdeveloped entrepreneurial infrastructure. Programs emphasising capacity building—such as seminars, incubators, and government-supported startup projects—may act as accelerators for releasing the entrepreneurial potential of the area.

Socio-political questions still add another level of complexity to the entrepreneurial terrain. The area has seen disturbances that can compromise company continuity, market access, and supply chains. Entrepreneurs must address these obstacles with resilience and adaptation, guaranteeing contingency preparations and operational flexibility. Although these ambiguities can be intimidating, they also present chances for companies who supply stability-oriented solutions. For example, logistics businesses that can overcome disruptions or digital markets by removing physical dependencies can find great success in such surroundings.

Notwithstanding these difficulties, Kashmir's unique socio-economic profile also offers different chances. Among the great treasures of the area are its natural riches, artistic creations, and rich cultural legacy. Entrepreneurs who match their projects with local capabilities and worldwide market needs can release steady development. For example, presenting Kashmiri art on digital media or creating luxury organic food goods with prominent provenance stories will draw attention from all around.

Recognising and meeting local populations' needs and ambitions also helps one understand the socio-economic context. Constructing businesses that create jobs, raise living conditions, and empower underprivileged populations can create a chain reaction of good changes. Entrepreneurs who see their companies as tools of social influence and profit-driven entities can help promote long-term sustainability and goodwill. Startups in Kashmir can overcome obstacles and help the area become a dynamic centre of innovation and opportunity by adopting a comprehensive awareness of the socio-economic scene.

The entrepreneurial potential of Kashmir depends mostly on its cultural diversity and geographical variation. Deeply ingrained in the region's identity, crafts, cuisine, and customs allow entrepreneurs to start real-world, creative companies. Startups can create goods appealing to local and international markets by combining modern designs with traditional Kashmiri aesthetics. Geography serves two purposes: although the area's natural beauty draws tourists and supplies for agriculture, its remoteness and rugged terrain provide logistical challenges. Entrepreneurs have to develop original ideas to overcome these obstacles, such as using digital tools to close supply chain management and market access gaps.

Furthermore, cultural elements like a strong feeling of identity and communal ties can be used to create businesses powered by the community. For example, cooperatives and social businesses can use the combined power of nearby areas to propel economic development while safeguarding cultural legacy. For those ready to meet the challenges of A Path Forward Kashmir, its unrealised potential presents a plethora of possibilities. Understanding the socio-economic situation of the area and using its geographical and cultural assets can help entrepreneurs build companies that propel social advancement and economic growth. Kashmir is ultimately a region of possibilities as much as of natural beauty. Entrepreneurs may unleash the great potential of this enchanted area with the correct strategies, support systems, and sustainability commitment, opening the path to a better and more prosperous future.

The backbone of Kashmir's entrepreneurial potential is its cultural diversity and geographical variety, which present a plethora of chances for businesses to combine innovation with legacy. The region's deep-rooted customs, food, and handcrafted goods offer startups an exceptional basis to produce products that appeal locally and internationally. Designing goods with traditional Kashmiri aesthetics for contemporary uses—such as fashion, home décor, or lifestyle products—allows entrepreneurs to profit from this legacy. For example, incorporating age-old Pashmina weaving or papier-mâché artistry into modern designs helps preserve these crafts and increases their appeal in global marketplaces.

Kashmir's geographical appeal, marked by its immaculate valleys, snow-capped mountains, and rich soil, lends still another element to its entrepreneurial scene. Millions of visitors annually are drawn to the natural beauty, which offers firms in eco-tourism, adventure travel, and sustainable hospitality-rich ground. Simultaneously, the area's rich soil and mild temperature help businesses in organic farming, herbal medicine, and high-value crops, including apples and saffron. Nonetheless, geography also presents difficulties. The remoteness and steep geography of the area often lead to logistical inefficiencies, making supply chain management and market access challenging for businesses. Overcoming these challenges calls for creative ideas, including using digital platforms for e-commerce, building localised distribution networks, or funding contemporary infrastructure to free traffic congestion.

Cultural elements further enhance the entrepreneurial ecosystem. An intense feeling of identification and community among Kashmiris can be used to support businesses powered by their community. By combining resources and fairly distributing earnings, cooperatives—for instance—can empower farmers and artists. While maintaining the cultural fabric of the area, social entrepreneurs anchored in communal ideals can assist in solving local issues, including unemployment and educational inequalities. These businesses promote long-term sustainability and social cohesiveness and stimulate economic growth.

Entrepreneurs who want to flourish have to take a sophisticated approach that fits their area's geographical and cultural reality for their business plans. This implies honouring and supporting the local way of life while bringing creativity that improves access to markets and output. In this sense, technology can be a transforming agent, linking Kashmiri companies with the world economy and thereby removing geographical obstacles. Examples of how technology may highlight the area's natural assets are initiatives, including digital marketing for tourism, mobile-based agricultural advice services, and virtual markets for handicrafts.

Case Studies

Dairy Farm of Shahzada

Through her prosperous dairy farm, 26-year-old entrepreneur Shahzada from Mitrigam village in Pulwama district has become a shining example for aspirant women entrepreneurs in Kashmir. Established five years ago with help from the Rural Development Department and a Self-Help Group (SHG) project, Shahzada started with only one cow. Today, Her farm has more than 20 cows, averaging 300 litres of milk daily, dispersed over four districts in South Kashmir and even reaches Srinagar, the capital. Shahzada, who only finished her education in the eighth grade, has shown extraordinary financial sense by carefully running the accounts on her farm and keeping exact records. Her path shows a significant change in her viewpoint on unemployment; she thinks young people may create their possibilities by starting businesses.

The goals of Shahzada go beyond milk output. Investing in cheese-making equipment will help her diversify her company and improve her product offers, reducing the epidemic's effects on the economy. However, she underlines the need for family and community support, especially for female entrepreneurs negotiating a typically male-dominated sector. Shahzada has effectively started her dairy company, but she has also underlined the necessity of more openness and responsibility in government support initiatives. She asks the Department of Animal and Sheep Husbandry to allocate resources and subsidies better to support neighbourhood businesses. With official numbers showing Pulwama will produce 31 crore liters of milk in 2020, the dairy industry there will be booming. Along with encouraging private businesses like Shahzada to develop dairy farms, this abundance has resulted in plans for five sizable milk processing facilities throughout the next ten years. The narrative of Shahzada shows how tenacity, creativity, and community support may empower women and propel agricultural sector economic development in Kashmir. Aspiring business owners can learn from her success since it shows that anyone can realize their ideas with the correct tools and attitude.

Amina's Farmhouse Poultry

Through her prosperous chicken farming business, Amina, a driven lady from the remote outskirts of Anantnag in Kashmir, has changed her life and those nearby. Amina, just 28 years old, started her chicken farm three years ago with help from nearby agricultural initiatives meant to promote women entrepreneurs. Amina began with a small flock of fifty birds and concentrated on producing native breeds known for their adaptability to the local severe climate. Using organic feed and putting biosecurity policies into effect to guarantee the health and output of her flock were among her committed to sustainable methods. Her farm has grown to house more than 200 birds over time, averaging 150 eggs she markets locally daily. Amina has not had an easy path. Her neighbourhood first showed mistrust of a woman running a farm. But her success has made her a model for other women in her community, motivating them to follow their aspirations. She regularly participates in community outreach, imparting her knowledge of chicken raising and encouraging other ladies to launch businesses. Amina has started looking at value-added goods like processed chicken and organic eggs to vary her income further. She has also indicated an interest in taking advantage of the Department of Animal Husbandsry's training courses to improve her marketing and poultry management techniques. Amina is still bright about the future despite the difficulties seasonal swings and market access bring. She thinks women can significantly boost Kashmir's agricultural sector with ongoing government assistance from programs and community networks. Amina's narrative shows how chicken farming may empower women financially and promote communal development simultaneously. Her dedication to environmentally friendly living and community involvement emphasizes the possibility of projects headed by women to bring about good changes in rural Kashmir.

Ladisha Techlabs Pvt LTD

Running Ladisha Techlabs Pvt LTD, an edu-tech firm assisting students in getting ready for competitive admission tests including CLAT, JEE, and NEET, Rauf Bashir is His trip emphasises political unrest and internet closures as well as the difficulties digital entrepreneurs in Kashmir experience. The Moneycontrol article on his attempts to alter opinions of Kashmir and establish a magnet for technological innovation has further specifics about his experiences. twelve

Kashmir: Hop On, Hop Off,

The open-roof bus trips of London motivated Suhail Rashid Shah's journey, Kashmir Hop On Hop Off. With this creative offering, he seeks to improve the travel experience in Kashmir. Although particular papers outlining his path were not included in the search results, his story captures the entrepreneurial energy developing in Kashmir's travel industry.

Meals on Wheels

Meals on Wheels, a mobile restaurant by Jeelani, addresses local dining tastes while negotiating social conventions by exhibiting innovation in the food industry. Though particular references confirming his narrative were not discovered in the search results, his entrepreneurial attempt shows the possibility of food-related businesses in Kashmir.

Bhat: Fashion Entrepreneurship

Bhat's path into fashion entrepreneurship shows how changing cultural views on women in business inside Kashmir are. While specific articles on her story were not included in the search results, her efforts reflect a growing trend of women pursuing entrepreneurial ambitions in traditionally conservative environments.

These case studies demonstrate entrepreneurs' unique challenges and opportunities in Kashmir, stressing persistence and innovation among socio-economic complications.

For those ready to negotiate Kashmir's hurdles, its untapped potential offers a canvas of possibilities. Entrepreneurs who value the geographical and cultural elements of the area while using innovative ideas can set the stage for explosive expansion. The area can become a vibrant entrepreneurial centre with the correct support systems—government policies promoting innovation, mentoring programs, and capital access—that enable change. Beyond only financial gains, this development can inspire fresh optimism and advancement in an area long defined by difficulties. Entrepreneurs who help unlock Kashmir's potential help their personal success and add to the more remarkable story of resiliency, creativity, and environmentally friendly development.

V

Cultivating an Entrepreneurial Spirit in Kashmir

Kashmir boasts a rich cultural legacy, stunning natural beauty, and continuing customs. But under the calm valleys and snow-capped mountains is a region with great unrealized economic promise. Connected initially with handcrafted goods, gardening, and tourism, Kashmir is seeing the younger, more audacious generation ready to change its socio-economic scene using entrepreneurship. This change towards entrepreneurship is not just a trend but also a required development in a country with great difficulties.

Value of Business Entrepreneurship

Entrepreneurship is now a force behind invention, economic development, and social change. Startups provide a road to empowerment and self-reliance in areas like Kashmir, where limited prospects and sociopolitical disturbances restrict traditional job markets. The entrepreneurial attitude helps people see issues, find answers, and benefit their local areas. Agents of change and entrepreneurs help close market gaps and stimulate invention.

For young people of Kashmir, business offers a chance to combine regional customs with worldwide trends. Young entrepreneurs can create sustainable economic projects benefiting not just themselves but the whole community by using the area's unique assets—such as its rich cultural legacy and natural resources.

Obstacles Affecting Kashmir Entrepreneurs

Even while entrepreneurship is becoming more and more popular, Kashmir's socio-economic situation provides various difficulties for would-be business owners to negotiate:

Restricted infrastructure—such as unstable electricity and insufficient transit systems—hinders company operations and market access. Many times, entrepreneurs battle logistical issues that compromise their scale capacity.

Access to Money: One of the biggest challenges facing Kashmir's entrepreneurs still is finding money. Often reluctant to engage with companies in conflict-torn regions, traditional lending organizations restrict startup funding availability.

Though the area has a supply of **trained workers**, there is sometimes a mismatch between the skills needed by different businesses and those there. Encouragement of entrepreneurship depends on closing this disparity using focused skill development programs.

Geographical and political circumstances might limit businesses' access to larger markets, restricting their capacity for expansion and attracting clients outside their own country.

Infrastructure Deficit

The infrastructure of Kashmir seriously complicates business activities. Typically, entrepreneurs deal with:

Restricted Internet connectivity: Business success in a growing digital world depends on dependable Internet connection. Many Kashmiri communities, meanwhile, have uneven internet access, which can impede e-commerce, online marketing, and customer and supplier communication.

Regular power outages Frequent power outages not only compromise daily living but also interfere with commercial operations. When power interruptions disturb their operation, entrepreneurs could find it challenging to keep output high and satisfy consumer needs.

Inadequate Transportation Systems Bad road conditions and few choices for transportation can make it challenging for companies to get supplies and deliver goods. This inefficiency could cause lower competitiveness and more expenses.

Capital Accessing financial resources is among the most critical difficulties Kashmiri entrepreneurs face:

Lack of a strong entrepreneurial ecosystem in venture capital Unlike more developed areas, Kashmir lacks a transparent venture capital system that might support entrepreneurs with money. The lack of investment choices restricts the capacity of entrepreneurs to grow their companies.

Restricted Knowledge of Government Programs: Many possible entrepreneurs are not aware of or find it difficult to negotiate even if different government programs exist to assist business. Their lack of knowledge can keep them from getting necessary financial help.

Market Access: Political unrest and geographic seclusion present obstacles for businesses trying to access more significant markets:

Geographic Isolation: Market access may be constrained in the area by its hilly topography and limited connection to main cities. Expanding a clientele outside of local marketplaces could prove problematic for entrepreneurs.

Lack of Useful Skills: Many young people have academic knowledge but lack practical experience in vital fields such as digital marketing, corporate management, and technology integration. This skill disparity can hamper their capacity to start and run profitable businesses.

Demand for specialized training: Targeted skill development programs that provide aspirant business owners with the capabilities they need to flourish in cutthroat markets are desperately needed to close this divide.

Risk-averse attitudes: In an area where conventional work is sometimes considered more stable, social pressure could exist against starting business endeavours. Those with a risk-averse mindset may deter others from launching their own companies.

Possibilities for Development

Notwithstanding these difficulties, it is becoming clear that creative and specialized business projects might help Kashmir harness its natural advantages:

Agriculture and Horticulture: Products with worldwide appeal, including apples, saffron, and walnuts abound in this area. However, insufficient technological integration and ineffective supply chains made much of their promise unrealized. Startups concentrating on contemporary farming techniques can maximize profitability and productivity.

Paddy Farming in Kashmir

Handicrafts: Kashmiri creations, including papier-mâché art and Pashmina shawls, have a significant market value. Many traditional artists, meanwhile, have no access to contemporary e-commerce systems or marketing outlets. While Kashmir has long been a popular tourist destination, there is significant room for innovation in sectors including eco-tourism, adventure tourism, and cultural tourism by bridging this gap. Startups that fit shifting global tastes can draw more guests and support sustainable living.

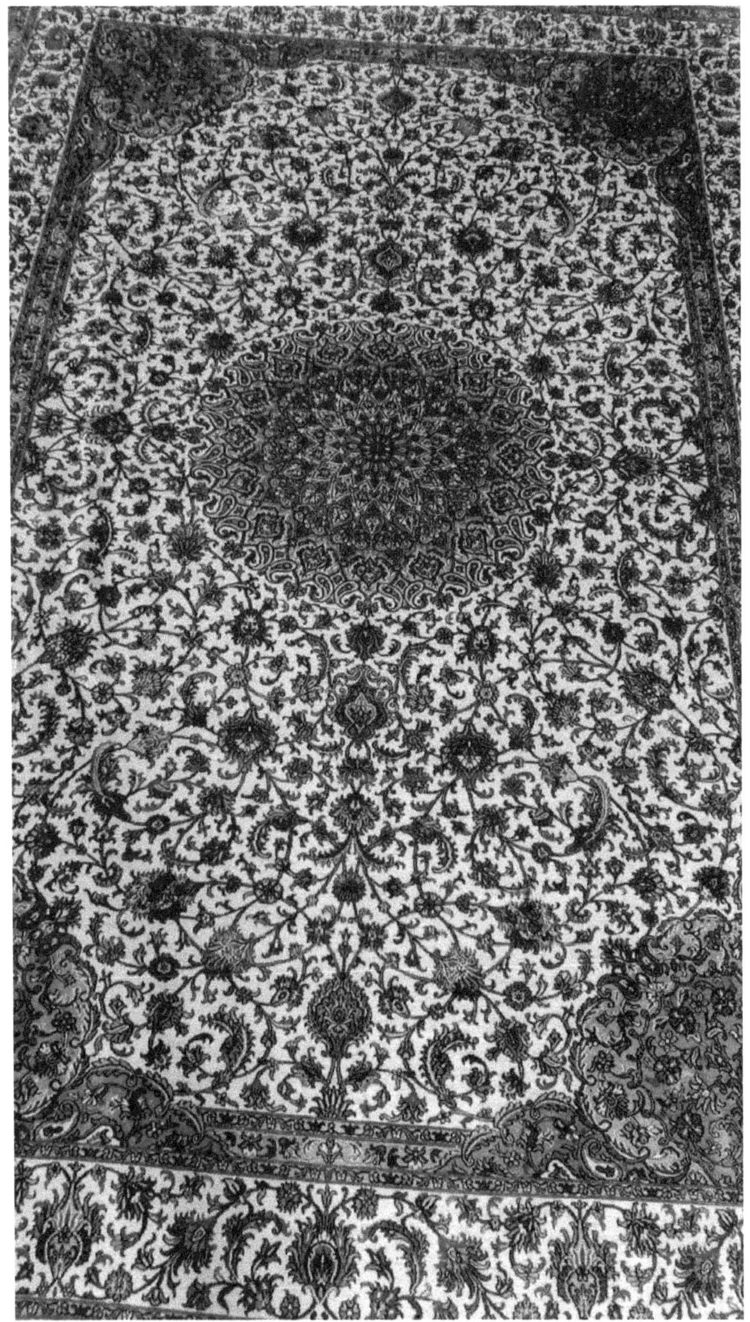

Kashmiri Carpet-Source: Elrex Trading

Government Programs Encouraging Business Creation

Understanding the power of entrepreneurship to propel economic growth, several government projects have been started to assist Kashmiri aspirant entrepreneurs:

Jammu and Kashmir Entrepreneurship Development Institute (JKEDI) offers necessary support through mentoring initiatives targeted at developing local talent, training programs, and financial help.

JKEDI's Role in Startups and Entrepreneurship

Fostering entrepreneurship and helping startups in the area mostly depends on the Jammu and Kashmir Entrepreneurship Development Institute (JKEDI). Established as a nodal organisation that carries out different government programs meant to support entrepreneurship, JKEDI is committed to building a dynamic environment that supports innovation and economic development.

Application of Startup Policies: First implemented in 2018 and revised in 2024, JKEDI is in charge of implementing the Startup Policy of Jammu & Kashmir. This policy seeks to develop young entrepreneurial brains using a framework comprising financial aid, mentoring, and training courses. Through well-defined policies and support systems, JKEDI guides future business owners through the challenges of launching and running a company.

One of JKEDI's main goals is to enable entrepreneurs' access to financial resources, guiding their mandate. These covers offering details on several government programs, grants, and funding sources, allowing business owners to get the required funds to start their projects. Reducing financial limitations helps JKEDI enable businesses to concentrate on development and creativity.

JKEDI plans many seminars, workshops, and mentoring events to give entrepreneurs fundamental knowledge and skills. Among several facets of corporate development, these projects address company planning, marketing strategy, financial management, and technology integration. By improving future business owners' skill sets, JKEDI promotes a culture of competency and confidence among startups.

Incubation Centres: JKEDI supports first-time entrepreneurs using incubation centres that offer a conducive atmosphere for startups to grow their ideas into profitable companies. These centres provide access to tools like office space, technological support, and industry expert networking possibilities. JKEDI enables startups to hone their goods and services before they hit the market by establishing a cooperative environment for invention.

Networking Prospectives: Between many participants in the entrepreneurial ecosystem—investors, mentors, service providers, and government agencies—JKEDI acts as a link. Using websites like StartupJK, an online forum for cooperation among several stakeholders, JKEDI promotes information sharing and development of partnerships. This interdependence fosters synergy among several actors, improving the startup ecosystem.

Programs for awareness: JKEDI runs awareness campaigns to teach people about entrepreneurship as a realistic career path to encourage and empower aspiring entrepreneurs. Targeting students and young professionals, these initiatives emphasise the need for invention and self-employment to promote economic development in Jammu & Kashmir.

Effect on the Startup Ecosystem

JKEDI's initiatives have greatly helped Jammu and Kashmir's entrepreneurial landscape to flourish. JKEDI has created a more favourable climate for corporate innovation by offering complete support systems that handle different difficulties experienced by startups—such as access to funding, skill development, and market entrance.

These projects have helped a lot of entrepreneurs from the area in many fields, including technology, agriculture, handicrafts, and tourism to surface. Among the young people of Kashmir, the entrepreneurial energy is slowly spreading and producing jobs and economic diversity.

Ultimately, the Jammu and Kashmir Entrepreneurship Development Institute (JKEDI) is vital in fostering entrepreneurship and helping local businesses. Using its multifarious strategy covering policy execution, financial support, training programs, incubation services, networking possibilities, and awareness campaigns, JKEDI fosters a strong entrepreneurial ecosystem in Jammu and Kashmir. More ambitious businesses are using these tools to help change the socioeconomic scene of the area and encourage innovation and sustainable development.

Government programs like the **Prime Minister's Employment Generation Program (PMEGP)** provide financial support and subsidies to promote regional startup activity.

Initiatives, including incubation centres, offer entrepreneurs wishing to enter the market workspace, mentoring, and financial access.

New Prospective Directions and Patterns

Notwithstanding these obstacles, Kashmir is seeing a quiet business revolution motivated by several elements creating a climate fit for startups:

Digital Transformation

Thanks to better internet connectivity and the explosion of cell phones, Kashmiri businesses can now reach worldwide via e-commerce and digital marketing channels. This digital change lets them get above conventional constraints related to access to a physical market.

Entrepreneurial Socialism

Many Kashmiri companies centre on tackling urgent societal concerns, including environmental sustainability, women's empowerment, and unemployment. These projects attain financial viability and help the community by matching corporate objectives with social effects.

Young-Led Discovery

With education and exposure to global trends, the younger generation is driving change in technology, fashion, and sustainable travel. Their creative ideas are changing the Kashmirian entrepreneurial scene.

Although Kashmir's fledgling entrepreneurs deal with significant infrastructure gaps, access to money, market access, skill development, and societal concerns, they also have a growing spirit of inventiveness and resiliency. Using new possibilities like digital transformation and social entrepreneurship, the young people of Kashmir can build successful companies that improve their financial situation and support more general socio-economic growth in their area. Notwithstanding Kashmir's particular challenges, there is hope for a thriving entrepreneurial ecosystem to grow with ongoing government backing and non-governmental organizations.

Achievements of Young Business Owners

Success tales that motivate others to venture into business help define entrepreneurial energy among the young people of Kashmir. Mehvish Mushtaq created "Dial Kashmir," a smartphone app with a thorough list of necessary local services. While residents and visitors depend on her creative approach, it has brought her respect and awards.

Starting "Kashmirica," a sustainable fashion company highlighting traditional Kashmiri artistry, Basit Bilal Khan Basit's endeavour not only empowers local talent but also emphasizes the possibility for expansion in industries like fashion and handicaps by supporting regional artists and conserving cultural legacy.

Noonley

Based in Kashmir, Noonley is a creative enterprise that has deftly modernized the traditional drink from the area. Founded by Saima Paul and her brother Zubair Paul, Noonley seeks to provide readily available Kashmiri tea in simple teabag and instant tea mix forms, enabling a larger audience to enjoy it. Along with honouring Kashmiri tea's rich cultural legacy, this project meets modern consumer tastes for simplicity and ease of preparation. The concept for Noonley came from a need to simplify customer preparation while bringing the authentic tastes of Kashmir to the world market. Usually requiring boiling, whisking, and adding different ingredients, traditional Nun Chai is renowned for its unusual taste and vivid pink hue. Noonley lets customers enjoy a cup of Kashmiri tea with little work by packaging this traditional beverage in teabags—just steep the teabag in hot water. Using academic knowledge in food innovation, the firm works with SKUAST-K (Sher-e-Kashmir University of Agricultural Sciences and Technology) to ensure their goods retain the authentic taste and quality connected with traditional Nun Chai. This cooperation shows a dedication to excellence and creativity, establishing Noonley as a leader in modernizing Kashmiri cuisine. Noonley is unique not only for its creative output but also for its support of Kashmir women's business. In a place where women may encounter social obstacles to business ownership, Saima Paul's path as a female entrepreneur is incredibly motivating. The successful Noonley launch by Saima inspires young women entrepreneurs by proving that combining innovation with history and supporting economic growth is feasible. Noonley has attracted good interest from the start for its distinctive offers. Not only are Kashmiri products accessible locally, but they are also finding their way into more general markets, therefore highlighting their worldwide potential. Social media channels like Instagram enabled Noonley to advertise its goods properly, interact with customers, and share its narrative. Looking ahead, Noonley wants to increase the range of products it offers and attract more consumers both here at home and abroad. Plans for more creativity and teamwork mean the startup will be critical in renewing interest in traditional Kashmiri beverages and promoting the local economy. Noonley is a shining example of how creativity may revive age-old customs and support small businesses. In addition to honouring their cultural legacy, Saima and Zubair Paul are opening doors for the next generations of Kashmiri entrepreneurs by turning Nun Chai into a readily available product for modern consumers. Noonley is evidence of the possibility of entrepreneurship propelling change and generating opportunities within the area as it develops.

Honorable Prime Minister of India Mr. Narendra Modi visiting
Noonley Stall in SKICC Kashmir

Noonley stall in SKICC Kashmir

Aisha: Changing Kashmir's Fashion Standard

Aisha, a University of Kashmir graduate, epitribes the tenacity of young women entrepreneurs in the area. Understanding the challenges of finding steady employment in both public and private sectors, she chose to turn her love of fashion into a profitable venture. Initially having difficulties from the COVID-19 epidemic, Aisha opened a boutique on the outskirts of Srinagar in 2021. But because of her family's support and relentless dedication, by 2022, her company started to grow. Aisha hires six designers today and serves various customers with modern designs and elegant phans—traditional long gowns. Her path shows personal achievement and encourages other Kashmiri women to follow their business aspirations.

Sakina: Overcoming Obstacles in Farmwork

Sakina is making significant progress in the usually male-dominated farming field in another part of Kashmir. As she negotiates the demands of this male-centric sector, her success narrative is one of tenacity and will. Sakina has started to inspire young women in the area who want to work in agriculture by adopting creative agricultural methods and environmental practices. Her path emphasizes the need for women to shatter stereotypes and change societal roles.

From Beekeeping Novice to Industry Innovator Nazim Nazir

From Pulwama, Nazim Nazir has turned his love of beekeeping into a profitable enterprise, causing ripples in the honey market. Originally an inquisitive enthusiast, Nazim overcame several obstacles through commitment and diligence. His dedication to sustainable development and excellence has helped him carve out a market niche and establish himself as a major player in the honey business of Jammu and Kashmir. The narrative of Nazim is an excellent illustration of how enthusiasm can propel a successful business.

Jibran Gulzar: The Forbes Nominee

Founded Gruits, a hyperlocal firm with headquarters in Jammu and Kashmir, Jibran Gulzar has become well-known for his creative method of using technology to link local companies with consumers. Jibran was nominated for the esteemed Forbes 30 Under 30 Asia List in 2023. Therefore, his efforts are not going unreported. His entrepreneurial path shows how technology can provide significant ideas for small businesses.

Hina Chaudhary: Championing Women's Empowerment

Another fantastic female entrepreneur who has dramatically changed the business scene in Kashmir is Hina Chaudhary. She works in the textile business and opened a first-of-its-kind clinic offering several beauty treatments catered especially for Kashmir women. Besides giving women access to high-quality services, Hina's endeavour generates employment possibilities for other neighbourhood members.

Omar Khan: Vision through Steel

The path Omar Farooq Khan took from a corporate job to start his own steel manufacturing company shows the force of passion and tenacity. Omar founded a company that has grown to be a major participant in the local market, having a clear vision for it. His success narrative emphasizes the possibility for expansion in conventional sectors when handled with creativity and will.

These narratives mirror a more significant trend of young Kashmiri inventiveness. Equipped with knowledge and exposure to global trends, young entrepreneurs are investigating many fields, including technology, environmentally friendly firms, and sustainable tourism.

The path to fostering an entrepreneurial attitude in Kashmir seems demanding and exciting. Young entrepreneurs open the path for sustainable economic development that can change the socio-economic scene of the area as they start investigating creative ideas anchored in local assets. "Startup Enterpruneship: Budding in Kashmir" this book seeks to highlight this path and offer practical analysis of more general entrepreneurial ideas. Kashmir may become a flourishing hub of entrepreneurship that survives locally and echoes worldwide by creating an atmosphere fit for innovation and helping aspirant entrepreneurs with tools and training.

Rich in cultural legacy and stunning scenery, Kashmir is also a hive of business activity. Many people have overcome obstacles to become successful entrepreneurs by proving tenacity and creativity. Here are some noteworthy success stories emphasizing Kashmir's entrepreneurial potential. These success stories from Kashmir show how entrepreneurs are overcoming significant obstacles—such as limited access to financing, infrastructure shortages, and sociopolitical unrest—to build powerful companies. Their travels not only motivate people in the area but also help to change the financial scene of Kashmir. More people choosing business gives optimism for sustainable development, honouring history and innovation.

VI
Agribusiness and AgriTech in Kashmir

Kashmir's economy has revolved chiefly around agriculture for millennia since its rich valleys and ideal temperatures produce some of the best food available worldwide. Kashmir's rich agricultural legacy and modernizing possibilities set it out as a possible centre for agribusiness and agri-tech developments. Entrepreneurs can revolutionize the industry by combining innovative technology with conventional farming methods, promoting sustainable livelihoods and accelerating economic growth.

1. Opportunities in saffron, apple farming, and organic produce.
Globally known for its superior saffron, apples, and a wide variety of organic vegetables is Kashmir. Not only are these agricultural goods evidence of the area's rich soil, but they also are the main engine of its economy. Though they have inherent value, inefficiencies in conventional farming techniques and supply chains and restricted worldwide reach have reduced their potential. This provides a rich ground for entrepreneurial engagement to propel development and creativity.

In Kashmir's **agricultural identity,saffron farming** is essential. Kashmiri saffron commands a premium worldwide because of its unparalleled perfume, flavour, and deep golden-red colour. Still, the sector has difficulties, including low yields and inadequate marketing campaigns. By using controlled-environment farming methods to increase output while guaranteeing constant quality, entrepreneurs may solve these problems. Furthermore, broadening the saffron industry from raw spice into value-added goods, including saffron teas, cosmetics products, and health supplements, will increase its financial influence. With clever branding, cooperative efforts with global distributors help market Kashmiri saffron as a luxury good everywhere.

Another pillar of Kashmir's agricultural scene is **apple growing;** the area generates more than 70% of India's apples. The industry suffers restrictions regarding storage, transportation, and worldwide competitiveness, notwithstanding its dominance. Modern infrastructure like Controlled Atmosphere (CA) storage facilities helps apples remain fresher, lowering post-harvest losses and allowing off-season sales. Entrepreneurs can also present blockchain-based traceability solutions to guarantee openness and increase consumer trust in the quality and source of the produce. Farmers may maximize their yields and reduce environmental impact by funding agri-tech developments such as innovative irrigation systems and disease prediction tools. With certificates and export-oriented branding, Kashmiri apples might be more noticeable on world marketplaces.

The expanding worldwide taste for **organic food** offers Kashmir another way for agribusiness innovation. The area is particularly fit for organic farming, given its relatively low levels of industrial contamination and large areas of arable land. Working closely with nearby farms, entrepreneurs can get organic certificates, increasing their output's value. Supported by adequate cold storage and logistics systems, establishing farm-to-table models can satisfy health-conscious consumers looking for traceable and environmentally friendly food choices. Furthermore, alliances with e-commerce sites enable the marketing of organic goods to a larger global audience and inside India.

Beyond these prospects, agri-tech's inclusion into Kashmir's agricultural system can transform sustainability and output. Innovative technology can help farmers maximize resources and make wise decisions using IoT-based systems for real-time data collecting, artificial intelligence-driven analytics for precision agriculture, and drone surveillance of crops. By providing agricultural advice services in local languages, mobile-based platforms help to close knowledge gaps and enable farmers to implement contemporary methods. Moreover, solar-powered irrigation systems and other renewable energy sources help to depend less on conventional energy sources, matching agriculture with sustainable practices.

Entrepreneurs entering the agriculture scene in Kashmir also have to deal with the infrastructure and logistical issues that have historically hampered its development. The first critical steps towards long-term success are building effective supply chains, forming farmer cooperatives, and pushing for government support through subsidies and policies catered to the area. Developing region-specific technologies and practices using cooperation with research institutes might propel even more advancement.

Overall, Kashmir's agriculture industry offers a rich creativity and business activity field. Entrepreneurs can release the great possibilities of this industry by redefining conventional methods via the prism of new technologies and world trends. Kashmir's economic scene will be improved, and its farm immunities will be raised if saffron farming, apple farming, and organic produce are also turned into globally competitive sectors. Combining vision, creativity, and tenacity, the area's agriculture can become a shining example of worldwide excellence and sustainable development.

2. Technology in agriculture.

Including technology in agriculture is transforming farming methods and making it a more profitable, sustainable, and efficient business. Adopting agri-tech technologies is progressively gathering steam in Kashmir, where agriculture is still a pillar of the economy. These technologies create fresh paths for development and competitiveness and solve long-standing problems. Using technologies such as artificial intelligence (AI), and the Internet of Things (IoT), Kashmiri farmers and businesspeople can reinvent conventional methods and establish the area as a pioneer in contemporary agriculture.

In precision farming, drones are transforming the field. With sensors and high-resolution cameras, drones can fly aerial surveys to evaluate crop conditions, spot insect infestations, and track irrigation coverage. Farmers may rapidly and effectively spot trouble areas with this bird's-eye perspective. Precision spraying of fertilizers and pesticides using drones guarantees that inputs are used where necessary. This focused approach lowers labour and expenses by stopping chemical misuse and lessening environmental effects.

Another transforming power in agriculture is artificial intelligence (AI). To offer practical insights, AI-powered systems examine enormous volumes of data—including soil composition, weather patterns, and past crop performance—in order. Predictive analytics, for example, lets farmers foresee weather changes, enabling them to organize irrigation and harvests better. Through picture identification, machine learning techniques can also detect early indicators of agricultural illnesses, facilitating quick intervention to save significant losses. Artificial intelligence provides a valuable risk reduction and yield maximization tool in areas like Kashmir, where erratic weather and limited resources are regular obstacles.

Real-time connectivity brought forth by the Internet of Things (IoT) has allowed farmers to manage agricultural operations more competently and reactively. IoT sensors for soil moisture and climate monitoring systems offer continuous data on field conditions. Automatically changing water use depends on sensor data, and innovative irrigation systems guarantee ideal hydration and help conserve water, a vital resource in agriculture. Similarly, temperature and humidity sensors in storage facilities help to keep perfect conditions for keeping products, lowering post-harvest losses. These technologies fit Kashmir's sustainability and resource economy demand very nicely.

By closing the distance between producers and markets, e-commerce sites are also helping Kashmiri farmers to be more empowered. Digital markets link farmers directly with consumers, distributors, and stores by bypassing intermediaries that typically erode profit margins. Farmers may reach a larger audience by selling their goods online, guaranteeing fair prices and improved returns. Small-scale farmers' mobile apps provide even more advantages, like access to training courses, market trends, and weather forecasts. Some sites also offer microloans and insurance products catering to agricultural requirements, enabling farmers to invest in technologies meant to increase output.

Unlocking Kashmir's agricultural potential depends on the harmony between ancient knowledge and modern technologies. Although cutting-edge technologies such as drones, artificial intelligence, and IoT provide creative answers, their integration has to be framed to fit the particular opportunities and problems of the area. For farmers to properly grasp and apply these technologies, for example, training courses are absolutely vital. Customized solutions can be developed and shared using partnerships with technology companies, government departments, and academic institutions.

The adoption of agri-tech technologies in Kashmir has broader consequences than only those of individual farms. These technologies help to achieve food security and general economic development by raising production, cutting waste, and enhancing market access. Moreover, applying sustainable methods fits with world environmental objectives, strengthening Kashmir's profile as a centre of environmentally friendly farming.

To sum up, including technology in Kashmir's agricultural scene is a need and a must for upcoming development. Powerful instruments that can solve conventional farming inefficiencies and create fresh chances for innovation and market expansion are drones, artificial intelligence, IoT, and e-commerce systems. Accepting these developments will help Kashmiri entrepreneurs and farmers turn their area into a shining example of contemporary, environmentally friendly farming.

3. **Expanding Value Chains in Agribusiness.**

The possibility of building value chains linking raw agricultural products to high-value items makes agriculture in Kashmir one of the most promising features. Along with improving the marketability of the produce from the area, this transformation process generates fresh economic prospects.

For instance, the apple business can diversify from sales of fresh fruit by manufacturing apple-based goods such as dried fruit, juices, and preserves. By establishing food processing facilities, one can significantly lower post-harvest losses—a frequent problem resulting from poor infrastructure for transportation and storage. Likewise, creating luxury products based on saffron—perfumes, wellness products, and premium cooking ingredients—may improve Kashmiri saffron's reputation internationally.

Value chains also contain certifications like organic or fair-trade labelling, branding, and ecological packaging ideas that appeal primarily to consumers abroad. Investors in these fields can enable Kashmiri businesses to distinguish out in cutthroat worldwide markets.

4. **Empowering Women in Agribusiness**

Agribusiness in Kashmir offers a unique chance to empower women, who have always been very important in agriculture and handicrafts. These initiatives can assist women go from passive consumers in the economy to active, empowered entrepreneurs by providing training in new farming technologies, marketing strategies, and financial literacy. Not only does this change support social transformation in the region but also economic development.

Women-led cooperatives concentrating on creating specialist products—such as artisanal food items, organic herbs, and traditional teas—can potentially become strong engines of rural development. Along with making financial possibilities, these cooperatives support the preservation of the area's traditional knowledge and cultural legacy. They give women a stage to display their work, access markets, and get higher prices for their goods. Women in these cooperatives can increase their negotiating strength and provide a more sustainable living for their communities by pooling resources and knowledge sharing.

Furthermore, helping women entrepreneurs is intensely focused on government programs and microfinancing projects. One of the main obstacles for women wishing to launch their own companies is usually access to reasonably priced cash and financing. These initiatives help women to invest in their businesses, buy required tools, and increase their activities by offering financial resources catered especially for them. Along with assisting women in the agricultural industry, this focused support motivates them to grow their companies, fostering more economic independence and empowerment. By emphasising inclusivity, Kashmir's agribusiness may propel social and economic development and a fairer and more prosperous future for women living there.

5. Export Possibilities and World Markets

Celebrated for their excellence, Kashmir's agricultural goods appeal greatly abroad. Entrepreneurs who want to seize this chance should concentrate on creating export-ready supply chains following international norms. This entails fulfilling strict standards and ensuring goods satisfy different regulatory needs and have reasonable prices.

Establishing alliances with overseas consumers and actively supporting trade fairs and events would help Kashmiri goods be more visible on world markets. For example, products like walnuts, honey, and saffron can be sold as upscale organic products to appeal to consumers all around who are health-conscious. These goods, well-known for their exceptional quality and distinctive features, can grab niche markets in rich countries where demand for accurate, premium, sustainably produced food is growing.

Export opportunities depend greatly on infrastructure developments, including better cold storage facilities and simplified customs processes. Especially for perishable items like fruits and vegetables, better cold storage facilities are necessary to preserve product quality and extend shelf life. Simplified customs processes help speed up the export process, lowering time delays and expenses that can discourage overseas consumers. Including digital tools like blockchain for traceability and certification improves openness, boosts customer confidence, and drives demand for

Kashmiri goods abroad. Agribusinesses in Kashmir can guarantee more consistent and sustainable development by spreading income sources and reducing dependency on the local market, supporting long-term economic growth.

5. Case Studies of Kashmir's Successful Agribusiness Start-ups
Driven by creative entrepreneurs using the unique agricultural resources of Kashmir and tackling local issues, the state's agribusiness industry is undergoing changes. These interesting case studies highlight several local successful agriculture startups.

Saffron Cultivation in Kashmir

Aquatic Farming in Kashmir

Mushroom Farming in Kashmir

Apple Planet Agri-Clinics:

From the Baramulla area, Ishfaq Bukhari has made significant progress tackling local farmers' problems through his Apple Planet Agri-Clinics.

Understanding the issues with the careless application of fertilizers and pesticides, Ishfaq rallied about 500 farmers to become members of his organization. Ishfaq's clinics provide various services, including crop planning and soil health management; his method recommends suitable amounts of agricultural inputs to improve crop output sustainably. He counselled farmers to substitute legumes for maize in apple orchards to lower scab incidence and raise soil nitrogen concentration. This creative approach made local farms more profitable and helped implement sustainable farming methods in the area. Many farmers' lives have been much enhanced by his initiatives, which also support environmentally sustainable farming methods.

Sabzar Nurseries:

Sabzar Nurseries, in the Budgam area, is a shining illustration of effective agri-entrepreneurship. Originally a private nursery, its main focus is growing and marketing premium plant saplings—including ornamental plants and fruit-bearing trees. Local farmers looking for quality planting materials now frequent the nursery; the founder's dedication to adopting cutting-edge horticultural techniques has helped Sabzar Nurseries flourish despite the area's climate difficulties. The nursery has dramatically raised its production capacity and product quality by using contemporary techniques such as controlled environment agriculture and tissue culture. This success narrative shows how local needs can be satisfied and sustainable commercial development resulting from agricultural innovation.

Farming Trout Fish

For young people like Irfan, who decided to start this business instead of a conventional job, trout fish farming presents an intriguing prospect in the Ramban district. Understanding the possibility of aquaculture in Kashmir's pure waters, Irfan started his trout farm, supporting local food security and giving him a steady income using environmentally friendly methods. He has maximized fish growth rates and guaranteed minimum environmental damage by using contemporary aquaculture methods and working with nearby fisheries experts. His success has motivated other young people to investigate aquaculture as a profitable business model, highlighting the possibilities for diversification inside Kashmir's agricultural industry.

Mian Nazim: revitalizing family orchards

By including modern agricultural techniques and diversifying output, law student Mian Nazim from Ganderbal has turned his family's traditional orchard into a profitable agribusiness enterprise. Understanding the market's shifting dynamics, he brought fresh fruit types and modern irrigation methods to improve output. Nazim's creative approach has produced higher yields and profitability for his family's orchard. Direct sales via farmers' markets and internet channels have helped him effectively reach consumers seeking locally grown, fresh food. His narrative shows how fresh businesses embracing innovation and market trend adaptation can help revive conventional agriculture methods.

These case studies show how creative entrepreneurs are tackling local problems and helping Kashmir's agricultural industry realize its unrealized potential, promoting economic development. From changing farming techniques to diversifying manufacturing processes, these people are opening the path for regional sustainable growth. Aspiring agripreneurs trying to make their mark in Kashmir's dynamic agricultural scene find motivation in their success tales.

VII

Tourism and Hospitality Ventures

Long a pillar of Kashmir's economy, tourism draws people with its stunning scenery, calm lakes, and snow-capped mountains. For decades, it has been a primary source of income and employment; nonetheless, the sector has had several difficulties, including environmental issues and sociopolitical unrest. This vital industry has to be revived and sustained by creative ideas, specialised products, and a strong dedication to sustainability combined.

1. Reviving Kashmir's tourism industry through innovation.

The tourism sector in Kashmir needs innovation to be revived. The scene has evolved as technology and changing travel tastes provide companies with fresh chances to offer original experiences and simplify the travel process. Entrepreneurs must be innovative to satisfy modern visitors' needs and set Kashmir apart as a top travel destination. These are some critical areas where creativity could change things:

Digital Tools:

Establishing digital platforms, including specialised travel applications and websites, would help visitors plan more efficiently. These sites can provide everything from hotel booking and guided trips to real-time updates on travel advice, weather, and local activities. Simplifying these elements will help Kashmir improve the visitor experience and facilitate safe and quick exploration of the area.

Including elements that let visitors interact with local guides or cultural emissaries will help improve their trip's authenticity. Using chatbots or live customer care, real-time communication can answer questions and offer tailored recommendations depending on visitor preferences.

Individualised encounters:

Customised travel packages allow tourism businesses to draw in particular consumers. These offerings range from wellness retreats emphasising yoga and meditation to gastronomic tours stressing native Kashmiri cuisine to heritage walks through historic areas, addressing specific interests and forging closer ties with the place. By serving these segments, Kashmir may increase customer satisfaction and attract a larger spectrum of visitors.

Sustainable Tourism Options: Travellers are prioritising sustainable tourism as environmental problems get more known worldwide. Startups can concentrate on environmentally friendly travel experiences that support environmental stewardship and conservation activities such as guided hikes, eco-lodges, and wildlife excursions. By matching these ideals, Kashmir can draw a more ethical tourist base and improve the local surroundings.

AR (Augmented Reality) and VR:

Virtual Tours: Without actually visiting Kashmir, providing virtual tours of its famous sites will allow guests to experience what the area offers. These virtual reality experiences can draw visitors to schedule their next trips by stressing the area's historical relevance, natural beauty, and cultural legacy. Virtual tours can also be utilised to provide historical background, such as highlighting local customs or antique buildings and enhancing the on-ground experience upon arrival of visitors.

AR can be utilised on-site to offer interactive information about historical monuments, point out hidden jewels, and design interesting surroundings that improve tourist experiences. AR software provides further details on a historic market or a classic Pahari mansion, enhancing the immersive and unforgettable experience.

By adopting these creative ideas, Kashmir's tourist sector may not only bounce back from previous mistakes but also flourish in a more competitive world. The secret is to change, use technology, and provide distinctive, unforgettable events highlighting what Kashmir offers.

2. Niche tourism: eco-tourism, adventure tourism, and cultural tourism.

Kashmir's varied topography and rich cultural legacy offer a unique chance to present the area as a top choice for specialised travel.

Entrepreneurs who satisfy certain hobbies and tastes might open fresh income sources and draw tourists seeking unique experiences. Here is a closer view of how every element might be used and developed:

Environmental Travel

Travellers who are more aware of their environmental impact and search for locations that prioritise conservation and sustainability are turning to eco-tourism more and more. Eco-tourism finds the perfect location in Kashmir because of its natural surroundings, varied ecosystems, and unspoiled sceneries. Here's how it might grow:

Ecologically friendly lodging:

Eco-Lodges and Homestays: Business owners can build environmentally friendly lodging meant to have a low impact on the surroundings. These include building with locally obtained resources, recycling trash, and running solar energy. Eco-lodges benefit nearby communities while offering an immersive experience where guests can stay next to nature. Homestays also allow visitors to experience traditional Kashmiri hospitality and culture personally, allowing them to live like residents.

Community Involvement: Helping residents with guided tours, trail maintenance, and cultural events is essential for environmentally friendly travel projects. Along with giving them another source of income, this helps people to feel proud of their natural and cultural legacy.

Guided nature walks, bird-watching trips, and wildlife safaris stressing local flora and fauna and conservation initiatives also reflect the approach. These encounters increase tourists' awareness of the need to preserve the natural beauty and uniqueness of Kashmir.

Trekking & Mountaineering Expeditions: Adventure tourism finds great possibilities in Kashmir's rocky terrain and picturesque mountains, such as those in the Pir Panjal and Great Himalayan ranges. From novices to experienced mountaineers, startups can plan guided hiking and mountaineering excursions to suit varying skill levels. These trips can call for excursions to far-off communities, star-based camping, and education about the native flora and wildlife.

Winter Sports: Gulmarg, Kashmir's famous winter sports location, is well known for its chances for skiing, snowboarding, and snowshoeing. To draw local and international snow aficionados, startups can provide equipment rentals, training courses, and guided trips. Snowshoe trips and cross-country skiing can also explore the area's less-travelled parts, fostering tremendous respect for the scenery.

Water Sports: Thrilling, kayaking, river rafting and stand-up paddleboarding abound from Kashmir's many rivers and immaculate lakes—like the Dal and Nigeen. To guarantee a safe and fun experience, entrepreneurs can plan guided water sports trips, supply safety gear, and arrange training courses. These events draw thrills and show Kashmir's natural beauty from another angle.

Travel for Culture

Heritage Tours: Kashmir's architectural marvels—including palaces, mosques, forts, and ancient temples—reflect its rich past. Entrepreneurs can create history tours that carry guests throughout these locations, offering historical background and narrative that vividly brings Kashmir's past to life. Along with visits to historic bazaars, which provide chances to buy handcrafted goods and engage with local artists, these trips might

Workshops in Traditional Crafts: The artists in the area are well-known for their ability to create complex handcrafts, including wood carving, papier-mâché work, and Pashmina shawls. Entrepreneurs can provide seminars where visitors might pick up these skills directly from expert artists. These events bring money for nearby artists and help guests have a closer relationship with Kashmir's cultural legacy.

Culinary Experiences: Unique delicacies include Wazwan, Yakhni, and Rogan, Josh, and endeavours abound in Kashmiri cuisine. Startups can plan food festivals, cooking lessons, and gastronomic tours, letting visitors sample authentic cuisine and learn about the local cooking customs. Visits to nearby markets allow participants to buy fresh foods and spices to keep as mementoes, augmenting these experiences.

Entrepreneurs in Kashmir can leverage a rising market of people looking for honest and meaningful experiences by creating specialist tourism sectors. This not only diversifies the local economy but also guarantees sustainable development and cultural preservation, assuring that the nearby populations share the advantages of tourism.

3. Strategies for sustainable tourism development.

The direction of Kashmir's tourism sector depends much on sustainability. The area needs to create plans combining environmental preservation, economic development, and cultural respect to bounce back and flourish. Sustainable travel methods can help Kashmir minimise adverse effects and assist local populations long-term. Here are the main approaches for advancing local, sustainable tourist growth:

Advocating Ecological Travel

The basis of responsible travel is teaching visitors about local customs, environmental preservation, and moral behaviour. This covers increasing awareness of honouring regional customs, cutting waste, and endorsing moral companies. Emphasising the need for responsible behaviour, travel firms, tour operators, and guides should inspire visitors to follow policies including cutting plastic consumption, honouring local customs, and respecting animals. Ethical travel information can be shared with domestic and foreign guests using seminars, pamphlets, and internet tools.

Offering tours with local guides who can offer insights into the area's history, culture, or environmental practices guarantees visitors an authentic and enriching experience. These guides can be emissaries, imparting to guests the value of sustainability and strengthening their bond with the location. Designed to reduce environmental impact and foster respect for Kashmir's natural and cultural legacy, guided excursions, nature treks, and historical tours can be planned.

Infrastructure Enhancement

- Investing in Eco-Friendly Infrastructure: Eco-friendly infrastructure is vital to meet rising tourist counts without endangering the surroundings. This includes creating trash management systems to lower littering, particularly in well-known tourist destinations. One can assist in controlling guest waste by using appropriate disposal systems and recycling initiatives. Solar and wind power, among other renewable energy sources, should be included in new and current hotels and tourist attractions. Furthermore, the establishment should have environmentally friendly lodging choices and eco-lodges to appeal to ecologically conscientious guests.
- Improving public transport systems that are both environmentally friendly and efficient will help to minimise carbon emissions, traffic congestion, and demand for private cars. While reducing environmental effects, well-kept roads, bike-sharing schemes, and electric vehicles can increase access to well-liked sites. Additionally, helping local businesses and giving visitors a more complete perspective of the region means building transport infrastructure that links rural areas with tourist centres.

Individual Involvement in Communities

- Involving Local Communities: Sustainable travel calls for active involvement of nearby areas. Communities engaged in tourism projects are more likely to support conservation efforts and economically gain from them. Residents' training initiatives can equip them to be guides, hostesses, or artists, generating sustainable livelihoods. This can call for seminars on entrepreneurship, language instruction, guiding principles, and hospitality. Including residents helps tourism become a vehicle for economic growth, supporting employment and income-generating possibilities and cultural preservation.
- Encouragement of social entrepreneurs with an eye towards cultural preservation, sustainable agriculture, and community tourism would help to boost the local economy. These businesses can provide distinctive goods and services, including cooking lessons, traditional crafts, and cultural events that reflect Kashmir's legacy. Social entrepreneurs can guarantee a more general distribution of the economic advantages of tourism by directly connecting it to local communities.

Support and Cooperation in Policies

- Effective, sustainable tourism development depends on the assistance and cooperation of local stakeholders, government agencies, and NGOs. Essential policies support sustainability, incentivise environmentally responsible behaviour, and safeguard natural resources. Funding sustainable tourism projects, creating certification systems for environmentally friendly companies, and enforcing laws prohibiting the overuse of natural resources can all be done in part by governments and NGOs.
- Giving subsidies, tax exemptions, and financial incentives to companies that follow sustainable practices will help to foster environmentally friendly firms. This might include backing for companies that cut water use, recycle trash, run renewable energy sources, and encourage community involvement. Working together, the public sector, NGOs, and businesses can create a strong support system that promotes sustainability and innovation in tourism.

Kashmir's travel and hotel industry has significant room for development and creativity. Entrepreneurs who embrace technology, concentrate on niche markets, and prioritise sustainability will help the area become a model of responsible travel. These businesses support the economy and protect Kashmir's beauty and legacy for subsequent generations. Sustainable tourism development in Kashmir will call for a coordinated effort covering the education of visitors, investments in environmentally friendly infrastructure, local community involvement, and policy support assurance. Following these guidelines will help the area provide visitors with distinctive experiences that benefit the local businesses and the surroundings.

Case Studies of Prominent Travel and Hospitality Projects in Kashmir

Rich in natural beauty and cultural legacy, Kashmir's tourist sector is seeing a rebirth thanks to creative businesses serving a range of consumer groups. Using exceptional possibilities in eco-tourism, adventure tourism, and cultural travel, local entrepreneurs are developing environmentally friendly business models. Here are some noteworthy case studies showing prosperous businesses in the hotel and tourism industries.

Green Valley Resort: Kashmir Eco-Tourism

Situated near Pahalgam, the Green Valley Resort is a shining example of an eco-tourism project stressing sustainability and offering a natural immersion experience. Established by local businessman Aamir Bashir, the resort provides eco-friendly lodging constructed from sustainable materials and activities, including guided nature walks, bird viewing, and organic farming experiences. It also supports local communities using responsible tourism practices that preserve the environment. Aamir's dedication to maintaining Kashmir's natural beauty has drawn environmentally minded visitors seeking real-life experiences. Working with nearby farms and artists helps the resort improve the guest experience and boost the local business.

Regency Hotel Pahalgam

In the heart of the Kashmir Valley, Regency Hotel Pahalgam is a refuge of luxury and elegance. Nestled next the beautiful Lidder River and surrounded by lush pine trees, the hotel provides visitors with the ideal fusion of contemporary conveniences with natural beauty. For visitors to Pahalgam, Regency Hotel offers a unique experience with its friendly welcome and well-appointed lodging. Travelers looking for peace, adventure, or both will find it perfect since of its strategic location close to important sites and calm atmosphere. The hotel's dedication to client pleasure has helped it to be a favored leisure and relaxation spot in Pahalgam.

Regency Hotel in Pahalgam, Kashmir

Adventure Tourism: Kashmir Mountain Adventure

Founded by adventure junkie Sameer Khan, Kashmir Mountain Adventure specialises in mountaineering, trekking, and other outdoor pursuits in Kashmir's breathtaking scenery. Seeing the rising demand for adventure tourism, Sameer started a business catering to thrill-seekers that guarantee environmental sustainability and safety. The company provides guided trips to well-known trekking paths, including the Great Lakes Trek and Kolahoi Glacier, giving visitors unforgettable experiences in magnificent surroundings. Sameer stresses the instruction of local guides to improve their knowledge of the nature and culture of the area. This strategy guarantees visitors real insights into Kashmir's rich legacy and creates job possibilities.

Cultural Tourism: Heritage House

Situated in Srinagar, the Heritage House is a cultural tourist project meant to expose guests to entirely Kashmiri customs and way of life. Established by cultural ambassador Zainab Malik, this business provides homestays in traditional Kashmiri homes (Dakhni Kothas) and gives guests chances to participate in local customs, cuisine, and crafts. Zainab plans workshops on traditional handicrafts, including Pashmina weaving and papier-mâché art, to enable visitors to learn from talented artists. The Heritage House encourages appreciation of Kashmiri customs through cultural interaction, generating a sustainable revenue source for nearby artists. Along with improving the visitor experience, this strategy aids in the preservation of the artistic legacy of the area.

Sustainable Hospitality: Hilltop Hotel

Near Gulmarg, Hotel Hilltop is a sustainable hotel that has embraced green ideas to reduce its influence on the surroundings. Run by Farooq Ahmad, an entrepreneur, the hotel uses waste management techniques, solar energy systems, and rainwater collection. Farooq's dedication to sustainability goes beyond infrastructure; he sources food locally from farms and supports organic produce within his restaurant. This method not only lessens carbon footprints but also helps nearby farming. Eco-aware guests looking for reasonably priced lodging without sacrificing their environmental principles have given Hotel Hilltop great comments.

These case studies show how creative Kashmiri entrepreneurs are renewing the travel sector with sustainable practices and distinctive offers. These businesses draw a varied spectrum of guests and help local businesses and communities by concentrating on eco-tourism, adventure tourism, and cultural events. These successful models provide blueprints for upcoming businesspeople wishing to leave their imprint on the dynamic tourism scene of Kashmir as the area continues to become a top travel destination.

VIII
Crafting a Legacy: Handicrafts and Artisanal Products

Kashmir's handicrafts and artistic creations are evidence of its rich cultural legacy and unmatched artistry. From the opulent Pashmina shawls to elaborate papier-mâché paintings, these works have enthralled consumers for ages. Meanwhile, the traditional craft industry struggles to meet customer expectations and modern marketplaces. Using creative approaches, revitalising these crafts guarantees their survival and releases excellent financial potential.

1. Revitalizing traditional crafts like Pashmina and papier-mâché.

The artists of Kashmir have inherited talents across many centuries. However, a lack of modernisation, competition from machine-made goods, and dwindling demand threaten many trades. Important areas for rejuvenation consist in:

Pashmina

Made from the pure cashmere wool of the Changthang goats native to the area, Pashmina shawls are known for their tenderness and warmth. Establishing geographical indication (GI) tags and certification systems is vital to stopping the rising flood of fake goods. These steps guarantee consumers get tangible goods and help Kashmiri Pashmina remain authentic. GI tags protect classic methods and improve the market value of authentic Pashmina goods, building consumer confidence and brand reputation.

Modern Marketing Strategies:

Digital marketing and e-commerce platforms can help Pashmina items be more visible worldwide. Using internet shopping, social media, and trade shows abroad, artists can personally interact with buyers and wholesalers. This strategy increases market reach and informs consumers of the painstaking artistry required in creating Pashmina shawls. Showcasing the artists at work via videos, online demos, and interactive sessions will help to value the product and draw attention to the talent and effort behind every piece.

Encouragement of design innovation is essential to guarantee that Pashmina items remain relevant in a cutthroat market. Maintaining the ancient Pashmina weaving techniques, artists can play with modern styles, colour palettes, and patterns that appeal to current tastes. Working with designers and fashion companies might result in limited-edition collections or unique partnerships combining modern fashion trends with traditional artistry, drawing in a younger, more fashion-forward audience.

Papier-mâché art

• **Increasing Product Range**: Papier-mâché art might be a main export good, distinguished for its vivid designs. Artists should vary the product line outside conventional decorative objects to increase appeal. This could contain valuable items, including picture frames, trays, jewellery boxes, attractive bowls, and even house décor items such as coasters and lamps. Expanding the product line helps papier-mâché artists draw a more extensive clientele, including corporate customers searching for distinctive, handcrafted goods, interior designers and event planners.

• **Global Market Penetration:** One must have a worldwide viewpoint to reach abroad markets. This entails knowing client preferences in several marketplaces and customising goods to satisfy those wants. Promoting Kashmir's papier-mâché goods to a worldwide audience can be accomplished by attending international art fairs, craft exhibits, and internet platforms targeted at artisanal goods. Working with foreign companies and designers can also provide fresh opportunities for a combination of classic and modern designs to be displayed.

• **Training and Skill Development**: One can use workshops and training initiatives to enable artists to embrace contemporary methods and enhance their talents. Improving the accuracy and intricacy of papier-mâché art could involve using stencils, computer-aided design tools, and templates.

Training in marketing, packing, and export documentation can help equip artists to satisfy the criteria of international trade, thereby assuring that their products look good and are professionally presented.

Copperware and walnut wood carving

• **Design Innovation**: Traditionally beautiful crafts with great cultural appeal are copperware and walnut wood carving. Artists must innovate their designs while maintaining the historic core to attract modern buyers. This could entail designing mixed-media works combining walnut wood with metal inlays or including contemporary geometric motifs and simple designs. New coatings and patinas allow artists to create goods that appeal to current interior design trends.

• **Marketing and Branding:** The success of walnut wood and copperware items in foreign markets depends on sound marketing plans. It is developing a strong brand identity that emphasises these goods‘ artistry, legacy, and cultural relevance. Content marketing, email newsletters, and social media promotions, among other digital marketing initiatives, can inform prospective consumers about the background and methodology of every work. Establishing an online business and engaging in digital markets would also help one reach a larger audience.

• **Forming alliances** with designers, distributors, and foreign stores will give artists access to more significant markets and fresh distribution channels. Unique product lines appealing to a worldwide market can result from cooperative efforts combining old knowledge with modern designs. These alliances can also help transfer knowledge, exposing artists to worldwide trends and modifying their creations.

Reviving Kashmir's traditional crafts requires a multifarious strategy combining modern corporate techniques with ancient talents. Artisans may guarantee the survival of Kashmir's rich cultural legacy while releasing great economic potential by keeping the authenticity of these crafts, broadening product offers, and welcoming innovation. Positioning Kashmiri handicrafts and handcrafted products as sought-after items in worldwide marketplaces would depend mainly on integrating technology, innovative marketing tactics, and international cooperation. Along with helping Kashmir's economic growth and cultural preservation, this revitalising initiative maintains the legacy of the artists from the area.

2. Modern marketing and e-commerce strategies.

Kashmiri artists and businesspeople must use current marketing and e-commerce techniques if they want to compete in today's worldwide market.

These techniques can enable them to differentiate their goods, attract a larger audience, and adequately compete in both domestic and foreign markets.

Online Media

Establishing online businesses on sites like Shopify, WooCommerce, or local markets catered for handicrafts can give Kashmiri artists a venue to highlight and market their creations. These sites simplify the management of businesses by providing security payment gates, inventory control, and shipping logistics, among other tools. Maintaining quality and profitability depends on artists having complete control over their branding, customer experience, and product pricing—all of which they have using a dedicated online store.

Working with global e-commerce platforms such as Etsy, Amazon Handmade, or Fair Trade websites will be helpful to attract worldwide buyers. These sites' customers actively search out distinctive, handcrafted, and artisanal items. Listing Kashmiri crafts on these websites raises awareness of a global audience, especially those seeking premium, culturally important objects. Using these sites helps artists reach new markets by connecting with a ready-made customer base that appreciates originality and artistry.

Social Media

Using Platforms Like Instagram and Pinterest: Social media provides Kashmiri artists with a potent weapon to share their works and narratives to a larger audience. Platforms like Instagram and Pinterest are wildly successful for visual storytelling, where excellent product photographs may draw attention and captivate possible consumers. Instagram allows artists to broadcast behind-the-scenes material, highlight manufacturing processes, and distribute client comments. This connects personally with the audience and fosters openness and genuineness regarding the artistry.

Establishing Niche Communities: Artisans can interact directly with possible consumers who are especially interested in traditional and cultural crafts by joining online organisations and communities centred on handicrafts and handcrafted products. Networking, sharing advice, and contacting buyers can be accomplished using Facebook groups, specialised forums, and hashtags honouring Kashmiri handicapings. This community-driven approach can also provide a forum for comments, reviews, and ideas, therefore helping to enhance goods and services.

Storytelling and branding

Creating a Strong Brand Identity: Kashmiri artists must establish a known brand to be unique internationally. This entails designing a logo, tagline, and consistent brand message that honours the historical and cultural value of their handicaps. The brand should tell its story by emphasising the artisan's legacy, talents, and conventional methods of creating every product. Especially in the online sales of items, a well-defined brand identity not only draws consumers but also builds trust and loyalty.

Sharing the Story Behind the Products: The emotional connection between artists and consumers made possible by storytelling is a potent marketing technique. Every item of Kashmiri handicraft has a narrative—that of the materials' source, the methods applied, or the cultural value inherent in it. Through blog entries, films, and social media caption sharing, craftspeople can inspire more respect for their works. A Pashmina shawl, for instance, can be sold as a sign of Kashmiri culture and history and a beautiful garment. Since they establish a closer relationship between the product and the customer, these narratives can help persuade customers to buy.

Work with Designers

Combining Traditional and Modern Aesthetics: Working with modern designers, we will produce original product lines combining contemporary aesthetics with traditional Kashmiri artistry. New ideas and trends brought to the table by designers can result in creative products appealing to younger, fashion-forward consumers. These partnerships can produce a gripping story combining the past and present to draw in a greater spectrum of clients. For example, a collaboration between a fashion designer and a traditional Pashmina weaver might produce a limited-edition collection highlighting the work's rich legacy and a modern, contemporary design.

Increasing Market Appeal: Designers sometimes have networks and may bring Kashmiri artists to fresh venues. High-end retail stores, foreign exhibits, and celebrity sponsorships that give the credibility and reputation of the craft can all be part of this. Working with globally visible designers helps Kashmiri artists raise awareness of their work beyond conventional craft markets and trade venues. This strategy increases sales and helps present Kashmiri handicaps as premium goods with a distinct cultural character.

Kashmiri artists may make their traditional crafts sought-after worldwide by adopting modern marketing and e-commerce techniques. These techniques enable a larger audience and provide chances for branding, narrative, and teamwork—qualities necessary for global market competition. Focussing on digital platforms, social media marketing, and good branding, Kashmiri crafts can develop from niche products to cultural icons that appeal to consumers all over.

3. Opportunities in the global handmade goods market.

Driven by a growing consumer taste for authentic, sustainable, and ethically created goods, the worldwide market for handcrafted and artisanal products is booming. Given their excellent quality and cultural value, Kashmiri crafts are positioned to satisfy this need. This industry offers unique chances for Kashmiri artists and businesses to profit from the worldwide trend towards handcrafted products.

Luxuriy Markets

High-end consumers increasingly seek distinctive, one-of-a-kind objects reflecting artistry and cultural legacy. Because of their traditional manufacturing techniques and uniqueness, Kashmiri crafts—such as Pashmina shawls, walnut wood carvings, and papier-mâché art—are perfect candidates for luxury branding. Highly sought-after in luxury markets, these goods provide a rare mix of quality, artistry, and cultural depth. Establishing Kashmiri crafts as luxury goods helps artists preserve traditional processes and increase their financial viability by commanding more sales.

Premium Pricing: The luxury market is about perceived worth as much as about exorbitant costs. Using the rich cultural legacy, natural dye techniques, and painstaking quality of the area, Kashmiri artists may present their creations as unique, premium items. One Pashmina shawl handcrafted with delicate embroidery and natural colours might be sold as a premium item combining modern elegance with legacy. This method guarantees economic advantages for artists, draws discriminating consumers, and helps preserve traditional talents.

Ecological and moral products

Consumer Priorities: There is a growing market for environmentally friendly and ethically manufactured goods as sustainability takes the front stage for customers. By stressing sustainable manufacturing techniques, Kashmiri artists might profit from this trend. This covers choosing environmentally friendly packaging, organic materials, and natural colours. Encouragement of such methods fits world consumer values and improves the marketability of Kashmiri handicaps. To guarantee low environmental impact, artists can carve walnut wood from nearby sources or use natural silk from traditional sericulture for textiles.

Improved marketability: Kashmiri artists may set their goods apart in a cutthroat worldwide market using sustainable production techniques. This can be especially enticing for consumers who want to prioritise ethical sourcing and environmental preservation. Furthermore, open marketing of these ideas helps customers develop trust since they are more conscious of their choices' effects on society and the environment.

Cultural Trade

• Global Interest in Kashmiri Culture: Growing global interest in Kashmiri culture offers a unique chance to design themed collections honouring the area's history. Craftspeople can create modern jewellery, home décor, and fashion accessories, including classic designs, symbols, and motifs in their works. These culturally inspired goods can appeal to a specialised market seeking distinctive, richly culturally significant objects with a narrative. For collectors, a collection of jewellery using traditional Kashmiri enamelling techniques or a range of home textiles, including complex papier-mâché patterns, can reflect the spirit of Kashmiri life and appeal.

Branding and Storytelling: By concentrating on cultural exports, Kashmiri artists can access a market that appreciates the stories and customs behind their creations and outward looks. Good branding and narrative that portray every product's artistry, background, and cultural relevance will help accomplish this. By telling these stories to a worldwide audience using digital platforms, social media, and influencer partnerships, artists may increase the apparent value of their goods.

Customised & Bespoke Orders

Custom and bespoke orders fit niche markets that appreciate unique things and personal experiences. Kashmiri artists can draw consumers looking for unique, one-of-a-kind goods by providing monogramming, custom embroidery, or tailored patterns. This could include gifts using traditional techniques, locally inspired decorations, or personalised Pashmina shawls. Custom orders let artists interact personally with consumers, create close bonds, and increase their clientele, thereby addressing personal preferences and enabling artists.

Using digital tools, including 3D modelling, virtual design consultants, and online order forms, can help simplify the process of producing tailored goods. By assisting artists to serve a worldwide audience, offering individualised services, and cutting the time and expenses connected with custom orders, they can also help each other. Kashmiri artists may increase their competitiveness worldwide and seize the rising desire for distinctive, personalised products by including these instruments in their business plans.

Reviving Kashmir's handicraft industry requires a multi-pronged strategy, including artists, businesspeople, legislators, and technology companies. The area can build a legacy that not only preserves its cultural legacy but also generates sustainable livelihoods for its artists by keeping old skills while welcoming innovation. With the correct techniques, Kashmiri handicaps will be brilliantly seen internationally, confirming their ageless attractiveness.

4. Case Studies

Pashmina shawls and papier-mâché, among other exquisite handicrafts from Kashmir, highlight the creative legacy of the area and present significant chances for business. These case studies illustrate successful companies in modern marketing techniques, revitalising old crafts, and leveraging the worldwide handmade goods market.

Elrex Trading

Renowned in Kashmir's handicap market, Elrex Trading has found a niche for themselves by fusing contemporary designs with traditional workmanship. Emphasizing premium hand-knotted carpets, the brand appeals to world tastes while highlighting the rich cultural legacy of the area. Using sustainable methods and local artists' talents, Elrex Trading has grown to represent excellence and creativity in the Kashmiri carpet sector. The brand has effectively broadened its market by mixing authenticity with modern appeal, therefore attracting both domestic and international consumers.

Kashmiri Carpet-Source: Elrex Trading

Pashmina Craft: Kani Shawl Weavers

Kani Shawl Weavers is a group of craftspeople dedicated to maintaining the centuries-old craft of Kani shawl weaving, producing beautiful shawls employing complex designs and excellent Pashmina wool. Combining traditional artistry with modern design sensibilities, this project has sparked interest in Kani shawls. The weavers have embraced creative marketing techniques by presenting their goods at international trade shows and using e-commerce channels to reach worldwide consumers. Emphasising their shawls' quality and originality has helped them establish themselves in the luxury market. This method not only preserves the livelihoods of nearby artists but also informs consumers on the cultural relevance of Kani shawls, increasing their worth.

Papier-mâché: Srinagar's Artisans

Initiatives spearheaded by local artists emphasising the creation of premium decorative objects such as vases, bowls, and complex wall art have helped Kashmir's papier-mâché craft flourish again. One prominent example is Kashmiri Papier-Mâché, a cooperative that assembles talented artisans to create original handcrafted goods. These artists have embraced digital marketing strategies to modernise their approach, including social media promotion and online sales via sites like Etsy. They draw a growing clientele interested in sustainable and handcrafted goods by stressing the environmentally friendly materials used and the work needed in producing each item. This change protects the old craft and provides artists with fresh means of money production.

Walnut Wood Carving: Ancestral Craftsmanship

Another booming industry displaying the area's artistic legacy is Kashmir Walnut Wood Carving. Craft craftspeople produce beautiful furniture, accents, and home décor using locally grown walnut wood. One successful business in this sector is Kashmir Walnut, which specialises in creating premium carved goods using traditional techniques. Kashmir Walnut has embraced modern marketing strategies to increase its market presence by working with interior designers to highlight its products in upscale markets and attending international shows. They also have a web store to serve clients all around. Their mix of modern marketing techniques with traditional artistry has helped them correctly enter the worldwide market for handcrafted goods.

Kashida Kari: Collective Embroidery

Initiated to revive the historic Kashida embroidery technique—which entails complex needlework on materials like shawls and clothing—Kashida Kari is Established by a group of Srinagar-based women artists; this collective aims to empower local women using skill development and market access. It uses contemporary marketing techniques using social media channels to highlight their work and narrate the background of every piece. To personally interact with possible consumers, they also show at craft fairs. Emphasising the cultural value of Kashida embroidery and its part in Kashmiri identity has helped them draw attention from national and international markets.

Through creative methods that combine legacy with current marketing techniques, these case studies show how Kashmiri entrepreneurs revitalise traditional crafts like Pashmina and papier-mâché. These artists honour their cultural past and grab profitable prospects in the worldwide handcrafted goods industry by using e-commerce sites and stressing sustainability. Their success stories highlight the possibility of expansion in the handicap industry in Kashmir, which will support community empowerment and economic development.

IX
Fashion and Tailoring Startups

Kashmiri apparel offers a mesmerising mix of its rich cultural legacy and changing modern styles. Rooted in centuries-old workmanship and aiming on the international scale, the fashion scene of this area presents great chances for creativity. From traditional clothing like the pheran to the integration of ecological techniques, Kashmiri fashion remarkably links the past and the present.

1. **Exploring Kashmiri traditional and modern fashion.**

Kashmiri fashion is really based on its strong cultural ties and creative legacy. Long a centre for workmanship, the area is well-known for its brilliant colours, fine fabrics, and complex embroidery. Modern influences have given these customs new ideas, so Kashmiri fashion is becoming more and more important in local and global markets.

Main Components of Kashmiri Style

Traditionally Made Clothing

Pheran: Men and women have long tunics called pherans, which define Kashmiri fashion. Showcasing complex embroidery styles including zari (metallic thread work) and sozni (needlework), it reflects Kashmir's ethnic character. Sleeker cuts, revised decorations, and global appeal modifications abound in modern pheran versions.

Shawls and Scarves: Kashmiri shawls—especially those produced from Pashmina and wool—are prized for their workmanship and vivid designs.

Though modern versions combine abstract designs and minimalistic aesthetics to suit different tastes, traditional designs including flower themes and paisley patterns predominate.

Fabrics and materials

o Pashmina and Wool: Still mainstays of Kashmiri design, these fabrics are renowned worldwide for their softness, warmth, and opulence. Time-honoured methods are used by artists to produce utilitarian and artistic scarves, shawls, and clothing.

Modern, daily wear is best suited for light, airy textiles with complex handwoven designs like silk and cotton blends. These materials let Kashmiri designers add dress, skirts, and other adaptable pieces to their line-of business.

Contemporary inspirations

Fusion of Styles: Kashmiri designers are keeping traditional themes while experimenting with contemporary cutting and forms. This entails accentuating woollen skirts with metallic elements or matching embroidered Kashmiri jackets with denim.

Global Appeal: Modern Kashmiri design is changing to satisfy needs elsewhere. Including geometric patterns, neutral colour palettes, and simple designs helps to create adaptable clothing fit for several markets.

Ecologically Conscious Fashion

Startups are emphasising on lowering environmental impact by means of waste-reducing strategies, sustainable fabrics, and organic dyes. This guarantees a low environmental impact while nevertheless preserving the core of conventional workmanship.

Fair Trade and Ethical Fashion: Fair pay for artists guarantees the preservation of their skills and offers them sustainable lives, therefore preserving their welfare.

Startups and Entrepreneurs' Prospectives

Combining Modernity with Customism

Startups can concentrate on creating collections combining modern fashion's utility and flair with the grace of traditional Kashmiri crafts. This can involve bringing Pashmina coats with modern styles or pherans fit for workplace wear.

Online Retail Systems

Entrepreneurs can open internet shopfronts to highlight Kashmiri design to a worldwide market. Digital channels can also be markets where artists directly market their works, therefore avoiding middlemen and keeping more of their earnings.

Entrepreneurs with a sustainability focus

Starting environmentally sensitive brands that emphasise the use of sustainable materials and ethical behaviour will appeal to the growing global number of consumers who are becoming more conscious of the surroundings.

Cooperation with Globally Designers

By helping to highlight Kashmiri talent and produce cross-cultural design advances, partnerships with foreign fashion designers can serve to exhibit Kashmiri work on world runways.

By combining its rich customs with contemporary sensibilities, Kashmiri fashion is ready to make a major impression on the world scene. Using its special legacy and emphasising innovation, sustainability, and internet connectivity, Kashmir may establish itself as a centre of premium, morally created fashion. Kashmiri fashion keeps changing, creating a legacy that links the past and the present whether through the ageless appeal of Pashmina shawls or the reinventions of the venerable pheran.

Startups in Kashmiri Fashion: Prospectives

Startups have a rich platform for creativity when Kashmir's rich cultural legacy combines with modern design trends. Using this synergy, entrepreneurs can diversify products, enter worldwide markets, and promote partnerships that introduce old craftsmanship to modern audiences while also preserving it.

Product diversity

Extending the Product Line

Startups can investigate a wide range of goods combining modern sensibility with Kashmiri design:

Revamping classic pherans into stylish, urban-friendly clothing; making bridal attire inspired from Kashmir; and creating seasonal collections utilising locally produced materials such Pashmina, silk, and wool.

Accessories: Including a varied selection of stoles, headscarves, and turbans featuring Kashmiri embroidery for both formal and informal events.

Home Décor: Inspired by Kashmiri designs, extending fashion ideas into handcrafted home goods like embroidered cushions, drapes, or table runners

Developing unique footwear lines with Kashmiri embroidery and striking jewellery pieces showcasing local themes or traditional silverwork.

Attracting Varied Markets

Targeting luxury consumers with unique, limited-edition collections stressing Kashmiri workmanship helps to

Younger, fashion-forward consumers may choose current designs mixed with historic components, such modern cutting or simple needlework.

Sustainable designs using natural dyes, organic textiles, and fair-trade techniques will appeal to environmentally conscious consumers.

Global Market Access and E-Commerce Transformation Digital

- Kashmiri fashion entrepreneurs can create a strong online presence to seize worldwide demand as internet buying becomes more popular:
- Establish e-commerce sites with immersive storytelling that highlight the background and workmanship of every good.
- Work with global markets such as Farfetch or ASOS to increase presence into premium and environmentally friendly fashion divisions.
- Use augmented reality (AR) technologies to provide virtual try-ons or highlight 360-degree product views, hence improving the online buying experience.

Luxury Branding: Emphasising the uniqueness and workmanship of goods like Pashmina shawls will draw in wealthy consumers searching for one-of-a-kind pieces.

Sustainable Fashion: Emphasising eco-friendly methods, including employing organic materials and biodegradable packaging, might appeal to a rising sector of ecologically concerned consumers.

Cultural Storytelling: Presenting Kashmiri fashion as wearable art—deeply ingrained in history—may establish an emotional connection with viewers all around who respect authenticity and culture.

Utilising Social Media and Influencers

Show Kashmiri fashion with aesthetically pleasing ads on Instagram, Pinterest, and TikHub.

Emphasise the adaptability of Kashmiri clothing in contemporary wardrobes by working with fashion bloggers and influencers, therefore generating attention on international fashion shows.

Cooperation and Sessions
Encouraging Local Craftsmen

- Work with expert artists to create one-of- a-kind products by combining modern styles with age-old techniques.
- Through the introduction of new techniques and materials, workshops help artists to innovate while safeguarding their special legacy.

Design and Interaction across Culture

- Form alliances with foreign designers to produce fusion collections appealing to a broad readership. For example, pherans with modern abstract patterns using Kashmiri scarves or with worldwide fashion trends.
- Organise cultural events whereby international artists visit Kashmir to learn from and work with regional artists, therefore promoting cross-cultural appreciation.

Training and Developing Skills

- Create design institutes in Kashmir to develop future talent and guarantee the survival of age-old knowledge.
- Provide ambitious designers and artists with entrepreneurship courses so they may learn marketing, branding, and e-commerce.

Startups in Kashmiri fashion sit at a junction between innovation and history. They may build a vibrant ecosystem that honours local artists and enthrals worldwide viewers by varying their product offers, adopting digital channels, and supporting partnerships. By stressing sustainability, diversity, and cultural preservation, these businesses may reimagine Kashmiri fashion such that it will inspire and excite for next generations.

2. Setting up bespoke tailoring and design businesses.
The Idea of Customised Tailoring

Offering clothing painstakingly created to match a person's specific measurements, stylistic choices, and needs, bespoke tailoring is the height of individualised design. Custom tailoring offers an unrivalled degree of uniqueness and attention to detail unlike ready-to-wear or even made-to-measure apparel. This strategy is perfect for consumers looking for unique, high-quality items since it allows companies trying to combine luxury with innovation.

Procedures for Establishing a Custom Tailoring Company

- Clearly define your niche.
- Choose whether your company will focus in men's suiting, women's couture or a unisex line.

Specialities: Emphasise particular looks such formal dress, bridal attire, casual cool, or traditional Kashmiri-inspired designs.

Cultural Fusion: Add Kashmiri design elements—such as Sozni embroidery or Pashmina accents—into contemporary fitted clothing to set a distinctive selling point.

Market Research:

- Investigate closely consumer preferences, rivals, and price policies in the bespoke fashion industry.
- Estimate first expenditures for tools, workspace, and labour as well as running expenses for fabric supply and marketing.
- Pricing policies should be based on material quality, customising possibilities, and service offers.

Get Customised Skills

Hire accomplished tailors with knowledge of exact measurement-taking, pattern-making, and garment building.

Training Programs: Provide seminars teaching your staff the newest methods in finishing, draping, and sewing.

Material Expertise: Gain thorough understanding of materials, especially opulent fabrics common in bespoke tailoring such cashmere, silk, and wool.

Location and Design: Select a site your desired customer base will find appealing. The studio need to radiate expertise and grace.

Modern tailoring tools, cutting tables, fitting rooms, and fabric displays will equip the studio to simplify processes.

Ambience: Set up a friendly, inviting space for fittings and consultations complete with mood boards and beverages.

Marketing and Branding

- Create a brand name, logo, and tagline that really capture customised luxury.
- Create a user-friendly website highlighting your offerings, portfolio, and client endorsements digitally. Provide online appointment scheduling capability.

Social Media Strategy: Share aesthetically pleasing material including behind-the-scenes tailoring techniques, fabric choices, and completed garment on sites like Instagram and Pinterest.

To get noticed, take part in fashion shows, cooperate with event coordinators, and network with local celebrities.

Client Invaction

One-on-one consultations allow you to personalise services by knowing clients' style and providing professional advise on cuts, colours, and fabrics.

Client Relationships: From design conversations to final fittings, have open lines of contact to foster confidence.

Loyalty Programs: Add free changes or discounts on next orders to honour returning clients.

Feedback Mechanisms: Continually hone your products by means of user comments, therefore pointing up areas needing development.

Developing Beyond Conventional Tailoring

- Once set up, the custom tailoring company can expand its products to include:
- Accessories that accentuate fitted clothing include handbags, scarves, and custom-made ties.

Workshops: Organising design and sewing courses to interact with the neighbourhood and provide extra income sources.

Cooperation: Working with nearby artists to include traditional Kashmiri handicaps into custom clothing will increase their cultural worth and originality.

A bespoke tailoring company in Kashmir can celebrate the rich legacy of the area and meet the increasing need for individualised fashion by combining creative business ideas with traditional workmanship.

Problems with Bespoke Tailoring

Competitiveness

Market Saturation: Both established companies and recent arrivals fight for consumer attention in the very competitive bespoke tailoring sector. Startups have to concentrate on providing extraordinary workmanship, original designs, and first-rate customer service if they are to stand out.

Developing a loyal customer base takes time and calls for constant quality and personalization—qualities needed to differentiate oneself from rivals.

Material and Labour Costs: While bespoke tailoring depends on high-quality materials and competent labour, this might increase manufacturing expenses. Startups have to combine keeping high quality with providing reasonable rates.

Rent for studio locations, marketing charges, and equipment costs adds to the financial pressure; so, effective planning and cost control become even more important.

Turns around time

Custom tailoring calls for complex work and several fittings, which might stretch manufacturing times. Managing expectations and preventing discontent with clients depend on open communication about delivery plans.

Scalability Challenges: Without efficient resource scalability, maintaining fast turnaround times while guaranteeing quality can become progressively challenging as demand increases.

3. Collaborating with global fashion markets.

Value of International Cooperation

For Kashmiri entrepreneurs, global cooperation presents a transforming possibility with access to a larger consumer base, exposure to foreign markets, and the possibility to combine several influences. Cooperation may increase brand awareness, inspire creativity, and help Kashmir become a major participant in the worldwide fashion scene.

Methodologies for Working with Worldwide Markets

Possible Companions

- Look for partnerships with foreign designers, stores, and influencers that appreciate cultural diversity and handcrafted workmanship.

- Create combined collections or campaigns combining modern global fashion trends with Kashmiri cultural aspects.

Cultural Understanding

Market Research: Know target markets' cultural tastes and style sense.

Adaptability: Customise collections to cater to the tastes and cultural quirks of foreign customers therefore guaranteeing relevance and appeal.

Fashion Week and Trade Shows

- Display collections in big worldwide fashion weeks and trade events to meet journalists, buyers, and influencers.
- Target major fashion cities including Paris, Milan, New York, and London to highlight Kashmiri workmanship to the globe.

Online Stores for E-Commerce

Use sites like Etsy, Farfetch, and Amazon Handmade to reach consumers all around.

To improve the consumer experience, provide international shipping, numerous language choices, and money conversion.

Social Media and Digital Marketing:

- Visual Storytelling: Emphasise the subtleties of Kashmiri fashion on Instagram and TikHub, including behind-the-scenes images of craftspeople working.
- Work with international fashion influencers to highlight collections and design interesting campaigns spanning larger audiences.

Advantages of world cooperation

Market diversification

- By entering global markets, one less depends on local demand and offers stability against regional economic swings.
- Different consumer tastes motivate creativity and result in original product offers.
- Cooperation improves brand awareness, so Kashmiri fashion is more appreciated and identifiable all around.
- Further strengthening the brand are more media coverage, celebrity sponsorships, and features in international fashion magazines.

Development and Learning

- Global best practices in design, manufacturing, and marketing help entrepreneurs hone their operations and products.
- Scalability and competitiveness are made possible by insights into supply chain management and market trends.

Difficulties in Worldwide Cooperation
Transport and Logistics and Shipping

- Global transactions can get complicated navigating customs rules, foreign shipping policies, and possible language problems.
- Maintaining client satisfaction and timely delivery depends on a strong logistics network being developed.

Cultural Variations

Misunderstandings in design tastes or business methods can develop. Overcoming these obstacles calls both effective communication and flexibility.

Pricing Strategy

In many different worldwide marketplaces, it is difficult to balance cost with the apparent worth of luxury, handcrafted products.

Kashmir's fashion and tailoring industry offers young businesses great chances to establish themselves both locally and internationally. Entrepreneurs can provide unique products by using the rich cultural legacy of the area, including ancient methods, and adopting modern corporate strategy. Working with worldwide fashion markets improves growth possibilities even more and helps entrepreneurs to present Kashmiri handicaps on a worldwide scene.

Maintaining success in this exciting and fulfilling sector will depend on juggling innovation with cultural preservation and negotiating obstacles including cost control, logistics, and competitiveness.

4. Case Studies of Kashmirian Fashion and Tailoring Startups

Driven by creative people who combine modern design with ancient workmanship, Kashmir's fashion scene is seeing a rebirth. These young businesses are not only bringing Kashmiri fashion back to life but also making a presence in international marketplaces. These interesting case studies show some local effective fashion and tailoring initiatives.

Poshak: A Tailoring Startup in Kashmir

Zari Poshak: Aiman Jehan's Boutique

Celebrated for its delicate tilla embroidery and bridal clothing, young entrepreneur Aiman Jehan launched Zari Poshak, a store in downtown Srinagar. Aiman has effectively built a brand that appeals to tradition and modernism by fusing Kashmir's rich cultural legacy with modern designs.. Customers at Zari Poshak can find a selection of goods, including elaborate hand tilla decorations on opulent materials, including velvet, silk, and wool at Zari Poshak The business specializes in bridal attire appealing to modern tastes and reflecting the grandeur of Kashmiri artistry. Aiman has positioned her brand as a go-to source for individuals looking for actual Kashmiri clothing by stressing quality and distinctive designs. Aiman's use of social media channels like Instagram, where she exhibits her works and interacts with a larger audience, also helps Zari Poshak to be successful. Her digital presence has allowed her access to national and international marketplaces, reaching consumers outside Kashmir. Aiman Jehan is dedicated to assisting local artists and advancing sustainable fashion practices even as Zari Poshak expands. Her narrative shows how young entrepreneurs could use cultural legacy to start profitable companies while promoting regional development and motivating the next generations.

Tulpalav: Online Fashion Revolution of Iqra Ahmad

Inspired by exhibiting ancient Kashmiri design mixed with current sensibilitiesation, Iqra Ahmad launched Tulpalav, the first online clothes retailer in Kashmir in 2015. Beginning with little money, Iqra used social media to reach consumers all around, concentrating on clothing like pherans, kurtas, and wedding gowns with Kashmiri embellishments. Her approach combines traditional techniques like Tilla embroidery with modern designs. Custom-made Tilla-work pheran, her most well-known product, has attracted a lot of interest both locally and abroad. Despite obstacles like internet shutdowns in Kashmir, Iqra has stayed strong. Tulpalav represents how an online platform can effectively promote Kashmiri culture while giving local artists sustainable livelihoods based on over 100 orders each month and a strong Instagram presence boasting thousands of followers. In order to match her online presence, she intends to create a physical store thereby strengthening Tulpalav's position in the fashion industry.

Pashmkaar: Honouring Kashmiri Workmanship

Focussing on Pashmina shawls and complex embroidery techniques like Aari and Sozni, Pashmkaar is a company committed to safeguarding the rich legacy of Kashmiri art. Established by Tariq, Pashmkaar stresses authenticity by using only pure Kashmiri materials and processes in its goods. By exporting its works to countries like the USA and the UK, the company has effectively positioned itself on the worldwide scene. Pashmkaar distinguishes itself from rivals who might combine materials or techniques by their dedication to preserving the purity of Kashmiri art. Tariq's vision is to ensure that every product sold under the Pashmkaar name reflects Kashmir's unique identity, which has resonated well with consumers seeking authentic handmade goods. Pashmkaar not only supports traditional crafts but also empowers local artists by means of fair trade practices.

Kashmir Loom: Modernity Weaving Tradition

Another interesting startup that aims to bring traditional weaving skills back in line with modern design trends is Kashmir Loom. Established by a group of young entrepreneurs driven by a passion for safeguarding Kashmir's textile legacy, Kashmir Loom specialises in handwoven textiles combining traditional patterns with contemporary designs. The startup uses e-commerce channels to reach consumers all around while supporting sustainable practices by sourcing materials locally and using local, trained artists. Consumers interested in ethical fashion have responded well to their dedication to authenticity and quality; Kashmir Loom aggressively shows their products at trade shows and events, therefore improving Kashmir's profile in the worldwide handcrafted goods scene. They are not only conserving priceless crafts but also generating fresh chances for artists by fusing innovation with history.

These case studies show how fashion and tailoring businesses in Kashmir are revitalising ancient crafts while adopting contemporary marketing techniques and worldwide prospects. By means of creative ideas, these business owners are not only safeguarding their cultural legacy but also generating sustainable livelihoods for nearby artists. Their success stories inspire next generations wishing to leave their imprint in the dynamic world of fashion and workmanship as they negotiate hurdles including market access and competition.

X

Technology and Digital Transformation

Software development, artificial intelligence (AI), and blockchain technologies present significant prospects in the fast-changing IT scene. These fields inspire creativity, revolutionize sectors, and generate maturities and entrepreneurial possibilities.

1. Opportunities in tech: software development, AI, and blockchain.

Software Development

At the centre of the digital economy, software development consists of designing, developing, and maintaining programs running modern companies and consumer technologies. As reliance on IoT, cloud computing, and mobile devices rises, so does the need for qualified developers.

In this discipline, there are:

· **Freelance and Contract Work:** Using sites like Upwork and Fiverr, developers can provide services worldwide, granting freedom and access to various jobs.

Emerging technologies, like machine learning, cybersecurity, and augmented reality, are fast-growing speciality areas. Developers in various disciplines can develop solutions catering to particular sectors, from healthcare to gaming.

Bubble and OutSystems are app dedemocratizing, allowing even non-programmers to create functional apps and enabling low-code and no-code development. This trend allows developers to build and personalize platform industries, profiting them.

Cross-platform Development: Applications running well on iOS and Android demand frameworks, including React Native and Flutter.

By modelling human intelligence to better decision-making, automate tasks, and enhance user experiences, artificial intelligence (AI) is revolutionizing interactive analytics to virtual assistants. Artificial intelligence uses are growing indispensable.

Significant artificial intelligence prospects include:

- Training AI systems to identify trends, make predictions, and inspire innovation depends on professionals adept in handling and interpreting vast datasets—data science and analytics.
- Companies that provide AI-as-a-Service—such as AWS, Microsoft Azure, and Google Cloud—have tools to enable their products to have AI capability. Developers focused on combining these offerings can uncover great value.

Automation and Optimization: ArtifiOptimizationgence-driven automation can simplify shipping, manufacturing, and customer service, among other sectors. Practical artificial intelligence applications include chatbots, robotic process automation (RPA), and inventory control systems.

As artificial intelligence proliferates, addressing ethical issues, including responsibility, privacy, and bias, is imperative. Roles emphasizing ethics, intelligence, and compliance will grow relevant to guaranteeing technology's fair and open application.

Blockchain Development

Blockchain is perfect for demanding openness, security, and trust since its distributed and tamper-proof character makes it Originally connected with cryptocurrency; blockchain has grown into spheres like supply chain management, finance, and identity validation.

Blockchain opportunities include:

Cryptocurrency Innovation: Rising cryptocurrencies like Bitcoin and Ethereum have created a tsunami of firms concentrated on crypto wallets, exchanges, and payment methods. Tokenomics and blockchain development experts are much sought after.

Blockchain improves efficiency and openness by allowing real-time tracking of commodities, therefore addressing supply chains. Companies, including agriculture and pharmaceuticals, use this technology to guarantee product authenticity and reduce waste.

Decentralized finance enabled via blockchain provides substitutes for conventional banking products, including lending, borrowing, and trading. Profiting from this expanding trend are developers and researchers focused on smart contracts and distributed apps (dApps).

Smart Contracts and Legal Technology: Blockchain lets self-executing contracts run free from middlemen. This transforms industries, including real estate, where automated property transfers are possible, and insurance, where claims processing can expedite.

Success in these tech fields requires ongoing education, flexibility, and a firm command of fundamental knowledge and new trends. Using these chances, people and companies may inspire creativity, tackle complex challenges, and create solutions that will define technology in the future.

2. Establishing a Digital-First Enterprise

Businesses must embrace a digital-first attitude if technology keeps developing to be relevant and competitive. A digital-first approach allows flawless operations, first-rate client experiences, and innovation by including technology in all business spheres. This is a detailed guide to creating and flourishing as a digital-first company.

Accepting Digital Evolution

Digital-first approaches give great client experiences across all online channels top priority. Companies must ensure their social media, applications, and websites are personalized and responsive. Real-time chat support, easy navigation, and customized recommendations significantly increase customer loyalty and happiness.

Understanding consumer behaviour, following industry trends, and enhancing operational efficiency depend on data analytics. From improving marketing efforts to spotting supply chain inefficiencies, tools including Google Analytics, Tableau, and CRM systems let companies make informed, strategic decisions.

Agility and Continuous Innovation: Companies must be agile as the digital terrain changes quickly. Promoting innovation and lifelong learning guarantees teams will soon adjust to changes in consumer tastes, technology developments, and new market possibilities.

Using Digital Platforms and Tools

- Digital-first companies depend on Slack, Zoom, Microsoft Teams, and Google Workspace platforms to promote teamwork, simplify communication, and effectively run projects, particularly in remote and hybrid work contexts.

- Online stores are essential for companies offering goods or services for sale. While payment gateways like Stripe, PayPal, and Square guarantee safe and seamless transactions, platforms like Shopify, WooCommerce, and BigCommerce allow easy establishment of e-commerce operations.

Powered by artificial intelligence, automation systems can manage daily chores, including:

- Virtual assistants and chatbots offer round-the-clock customer service.
- AI-driven systems track stock levels and maximize procurement-maximize guiding inventory management.
- Automated processes speed up operations and help to lower hand-made mistakes.
- Cloud-based services—such as AWS, Microsoft Azure, and Google Cloud—offer scalability and flexibility that let companies run apps, save data, and access resources from anywhere.
- Using Global Remote Work Opportunities for Local Talent The worldwide move to remote work has removed many geographical restrictions, allowing companies to draw on worldwide talent pools and give local professionals access to abroad prospects.

Benefits of Remote Work for Local Talent Access to Worldwide Opportunities:

- For local experts, remote employment provides access to highly paid overseas positions that let them engage in projects with top-notch multinational corporations without moving.
- Working with multinational teams exposes local talent to innovative technology, varied approaches, and cross-cultural cooperation, enhancing skills development—certifications and chances for online learning help to improve their competencies even more.
- **Work-Life Balance:** The freedom of remote work lets people balance personal and professional obligations, raising their satisfaction and output.
- Businesses employing local remote talent help the local economy by offering consistent income and chances for career advancement, promoting regional development.

Problems and Solutions for Remote Work
Coordinating Time Zones:

- Time zone variances can complicate communication and scheduling. Among the solutions are asynchronous communication technologies like Notion or Slack and well-established procedures that let team members effectively operate across several time zones.
- Cultural variances can influence team dynamics. Honest communication and training in cultural awareness help build understanding and cooperation.
- Remote working calls for strong cybersecurity policies, including:
- Mandating VPN use for safe access.
- Applying multi-factor security.
- Having frequent cybersecurity best practices training courses.

Establishing a digital-first company is about building an ecosystem using technology to support development, efficiency, and customer happiness, not only about using new technologies. Businesses might flourish in a world growingly linked by embracing digital transformation, using the correct platforms, and grabbing worldwide prospects. In the digital era, people with digital abilities can gain from more job marketplaces and further education, generating a win-win situation.

4. Case Studies

Despite particular obstacles, including political unrest and poor internet access, Kashmir is becoming a growing centre for technology and digital transformation. Local entrepreneurs are building significant companies using possibilities in software development, artificial intelligence (AI), and blockchain technology. These noteworthy case studies show the promise of tech businesses in Kashmir.

Ladisha Techlabs:

Founded by Rauf Bashir, Ladisha Techlabs is an edu-tech firm seeking to assist students in getting ready for demanding admission tests, including CLAT, JEE, and NEET. Launched in 2016, the firm responds to the high unemployment rate in Jammu and Kashmir, which has prompted many young people to pursue educational possibilities outside the region. Despite significant obstacles, Rauf is dedicated to his goal, which includes regular internet blackouts and insufficient local enthusiasm for technological education. Having invested about ₹6 lakh, he has bootstrapped the business and concentrated on building a digital platform using internet resources to support learning. Rauf has had to negotiate systematic hazards and a lack of assistance from the local ecology on his path. However, his will to establish an incubation space in Kashmir captures the developing entrepreneurial energy in the area. Ladisha Techlabs shows how tech companies may meet local educational requirements and give young people chances to be empowered via digital learning tools. One can find:

FastBeetle

Using technology to simplify delivery systems, FastBeetle—a logistics startup—has become popular in Jammu and Kashmir. Initially founded by young entrepreneurs, FastBeetle provides an app-based network linking consumers with nearby delivery companies for various goods, including food and basics. Especially during the COVID-19 epidemic, when internet buying exploded, the firm profited from the increased need for effective logistical solutions. FastBeetle creates employment in the local community by using local delivery agents who receive training on using the app efficiently. FastBeetle has drawn over 70,000 users in a short period by concentrating on dependability and user experience. The company shows how technology may improve service delivery in areas with particular logistical difficulties and promote economic development using job creation. 6. Kashmir Angel Network: Backing Local Entrepreneurs

Kashmir Angel Network

An effort aiming at encouraging entrepreneurship by matching nearby businesses with investors is the Kashmir Angel Network. Designed to close the financing gap experienced by local digital companies, this network consists of angel investors ready to support exciting businesses. The network is crucial in helping companies in their early years by offering financial support, mentoring, and direction. The Kashmir Angel Network enables local companies to get the required funding to scale their operations using contacts between entrepreneurs and investors outside Kashmir. This project emphasizes the need to create a conducive environment for technologically advanced companies in Kashmir so they may flourish despite outside difficulties.

Czar

Czar is a blockchain-based enterprise aimed at offering creative ideas to local businesses in Kashmir. Initially founded by tech aficionados, Czar aims to create distributed apps (dApps), improving security and openness for several industries, including supply chain management and agriculture.

Using blockchain technology, Czar tackles problems, including inefficiencies in conventional corporate models and fraud. The solutions of the startup enable local companies to use contemporary technologies while guaranteeing data security and integrity. Although potential customers first struggle with awareness and knowledge of blockchain technology, Czar has effectively shown its value proposition through trial projects showing more efficiency and lower costs for involved companies. Second:

These case studies show how Kashmiri businesspeople use digital transformation and technology to develop creative ideas addressing local problems. From Ladisha Techlabs' educational platforms to logistics companies like FastBeetle and blockchain projects like Czar, these companies show promise for expansion inside Kashmir's digital scene. The area will likely become a major participant in India's startup scene as more business owners take advantage of worldwide remote work possibilities and technology developments.

XI

Overcoming Challenges and Sustaining Growth

Establishing and keeping a profitable company in Kashmir calls for tenacity, flexibility, and a thorough awareness of the area's particular difficulties. Operating hazards, resource constraints, and socio-political uncertainty require a deliberate approach to guarantee stability and long-term development. Entrepreneurs must concentrate on risk reduction, community involvement, and creative application to negotiate these obstacles properly.

1. Navigating socio-political challenges and uncertainty

Entrepreneurs have to grasp the area's historical background and how it affects the local business. Developing plans to fit unforeseen developments depends on a comprehensive awareness of the political and legal surroundings.

Dealing with local authorities and keeping current on government policies will help to provide business planning direction and clarity. Using projects like recruiting local talent, supporting community development programs, or working with local suppliers, entrepreneurs should also aim to establish close ties with nearby communities, so displaying their devotion. These initiatives not only generate goodwill but also create a supportive network that can help to give stability in difficult times.

Building a Resilient Operational Framework

Businesses that want to survive against any interruptions have to give risk management top priority. The creation of a crisis management strategy is vital. Such a strategy should specify procedures for protecting staff, safeguarding assets, and keeping lines of contact open to stakeholders under duress. Purchasing insurance specifically for local hazards—covering property damage or supply chain interruptions—offers a safety net for unanticipated circumstances.

Diversification

Entrepreneurs can lessen dependency on local markets by broadening their products to appeal to national or worldwide consumers. Geographic diversification—establishing activities in more stable areas—can also help companies to keep a presence in Kashmir by reducing risks.

Accepting Technology and Originality

Overcoming many of the problems in the area depends on technology. Using digital solutions like e-commerce sites will enable companies to enter markets outside of Kashmir, therefore guaranteeing consistent income even during local interruptions. Cloud-based systems help with safe data storage and remote access when physical access to corporate sites is limited.

AI-driven tools and automation help maximize operations, lowering reliance on human labour during workforce absence. For instance, automated customer service bots and inventory control can keep efficiency while freeing funds for other company departments.

Using Local and Worldwide Networks

Resilience and development can both benefit much from cooperation. Working with nearby companies, artists, and suppliers creates a linked ecosystem supporting individual achievement. Engaging with worldwide networks simultaneously might provide access to mentoring, financing possibilities, and new markets. Engaging in trade exhibits or forming alliances with foreign companies lets companies highlight their goods and draw different customer bases.

Participating with non-governmental and governmental groups also grants access to more resources. These alliances can reduce the load of working in demanding surroundings by providing technical support, financial incentives, or infrastructure help.

Creating a Culture of Flexibility

Maintaining development under uncertain circumstances depends on a strong corporate culture. Employees should feel encouraged and appreciated since their devotion and morale directly affect company success. Providing mental health tools, professional growth chances, and open contact lines will help produce a motivated and strong team.

Businesspeople should create surroundings that inspire creativity and flexibility. Companies that enable staff members to provide ideas and solutions will be ahead of industry trends and evolving conditions. Constant learning guarantees the staff is ready to meet challenges and seize fresh prospects.

Giving sustainability a top priority

For companies all over, sustainability is becoming increasingly important, and it is especially relevant in Kashmir. Using sustainable materials, cutting waste, and using energy-efficient manufacturing techniques might draw investors and consumers who share environmental concerns. Fairtrade policies help nearby suppliers and artists establish relationships with the community and improve the company's reputation.

Companies can also foster more general community growth by investing in sectors including infrastructure, healthcare, or education. These initiatives not only raise the general standard of living in the area but also support the business's responsibility as a constructive agent in society.

Keeping a Long-Term View

Although working in Kashmir has definite difficulties, the area also provides unique chances for development and creativity. Those who see the long run and concentrate on creating strong and flexible companies will flourish despite the uncertainty. Businesses may help the area's economic growth by using technology, encouraging teamwork, and prioritizing sustainability. This will have a long-lasting effect.

Overcoming obstacles and maintaining development calls for tenacity, ingenuity, and a dedication to continually improving. Kashmiri entrepreneurs have the power to bring about significant transformation for the communities they serve and their companies.

2. Building resilience and managing risks.

Especially in the complicated surroundings of Kashmir, entrepreneurial success calls for tenacity and good risk management. Risk management protects companies' stability and future expansion; resilience helps them to meet obstacles. These elements, taken together, give a basis for negotiating uncertainty and grabbing possibilities in a market that is always changing.

Developing Resilience

In business, resilience is agility, capacity building, and using creativity to survive and flourish in adversity. Entrepreneurs have to be adaptable if they want long-term viability. Agility helps companies to adapt to changes in consumer preferences, industry conditions, and unanticipated events. This could mean changing marketing plans, business models, or supply chain configurations to stay competitive.

Resilience also depends critically on investments in human resources. Training and skill development chances given to staff members help companies create an innovative and always learning culture. Encouragement of employees inside the company improves output and generates a workforce fit for handling fresh problems.

Technology strengthens resilience significantly. Digital tools promote data-driven decision-making, enhance communication, and help to simplify processes. Analytics lets entrepreneurs spot patterns, streamline procedures, and project changes in the market. Furthermore, creating creative goods and services that fit changing consumer wants guarantees a company stays competitive and relevant.

Handling Risks

Maintaining corporate activities and expansion depends on risk management. A pillar of risk control is good financial planning since it guarantees consistency in uncertain times. Businesses that keep good cash flow, protect credit lines, and get ready for unanticipated costs will be able to weather economic swings. By diversifying assets and investments, one less depends on a single income source and distributes financial risks.

Monitoring and assessment systems help companies evaluate their performance and find any weaknesses. Regularly reviewing operational data and market situations allows one to be proactive and solve developing problems before they become more serious. Developing a crisis communication plan guarantees that stakeholders—including staff, consumers, and investors—receive accurate and timely information in times of disturbance, therefore maintaining confidence and reducing harm to reputation.

Diversification provides a barrier against localized hazards as well. Expanding product or service offers, breaking into new markets, or using other business strategies will help companies escape the effects of regional instability. To reduce risks even further, entrepreneurs should look at joint ventures with suppliers and partners outside their vicinity.

3. Scaling your business: taking it from local to global.

From a small local firm to a worldwide one, scaling a company offers unique difficulties and outstanding development possibilities. Kashmir's entrepreneurs can use the worldwide need for unique goods and services to reach other countries.

Effective expansion starts with thorough market research. Knowing consumer preferences, legal rules, and competition in target markets offers an insightful analysis that helps one make decisions. Efforts at cultural sensitivity and localization are just as vital. Customizing goods, services, and marketing plans to fit regional cultures and customer behaviour increases credibility and acceptability.

Strategic alliances help to smooth the way one enters worldwide marketplaces. Working with local firms or foreign corporations gives access to resources, proven distribution channels, and experience. While increasing the company's footprint, joint ventures or franchising agreements help lower operating risks.

Globally, scaling calls for careful financial thinking. Getting money for growth could call for looking at grants, loans, angel investors, or venture capital. Entrepreneurs should consider currency risks and apply financial instruments such as hedging or foreign exchange accounts to balance international transactions.

Constant observation and adaption guarantee ongoing success in emerging markets. Tracking sales, customer comments, and industry trends helps companies to modify their plans better and react to changes. Maintaining relevance and competitiveness depends on a readiness to change course and invent in response to the global market dynamics.

Sustainable Development

Risk management and resilience are continuous activities, not one-time endeavours. Entrepreneurs must continually evaluate and adjust their plans to fit new conditions. Businesses can negotiate obstacles and attain sustainable development by encouraging a strong organizational culture, welcoming innovation, and applying sound risk management techniques.

In Kashmir specifically, these strategies are helpful. Builders of firm operations and strategic risk management succeed in the local market and scale their companies worldwide, promoting economic growth and generating long-lasting influence.

Entrepreneurship expresses the vision, resiliency, and the will to produce significant influence, not only a quest for profit. Emphasizing the qualities, attitudes, and values that define success in the face of adversity, this book has travelled to the core of what it means to be an entrepreneur in a fast-changing environment. From concept to execution, the entrepreneurial path is one of transformation—from ideas into reality by tenacity, strategy, and adaptation. From accelerators to digital tools, the ecosystem supporting this path is as important as the goal since it provides resources and networks to foster development.

Within Kashmir's exceptional and unrealized potential, entrepreneurship becomes a tremendous weapon for transformation. Even while sociopolitical obstacles try the will of businesses, its socioeconomic scene, rich culture, and varied resources provide a rich ground for creativity. Agribusiness, tourism, handicap crafts, and technology are among the many possibilities just waiting to be seized. From using e-commerce to cutting-edge technologies, the mix of history with current ideas shows how Kashmir's businesses may interact with worldwide markets while maintaining their character.

One shining example of hope throughout this research is the resiliency of Kashmiri entrepreneurs. Navigating uncertainty with bravery and dedication to their mission, they adapt, invent, and tenaciously continue. Whether revamping the tourism sector, scaling agriculture companies, or embracing digital change, these trailblazers are rewriting the story of their native country and opening paths to social empowerment and economic development.

Ultimately, entrepreneurship is about creating legacies, not only about starting companies. It's the will to leave a lasting impression, to help the world, and to produce something timeless. This path is evidence of the transforming power of ideas, the strength of resiliency, and the countless opportunities for human innovation for Kashmiri and beyond entrepreneurs. Let this book remind you as you go into your entrepreneurial road that, despite obstacles, the possibilities for development, creativity, and influence are almost endless. Though the road is never easy, it is always well worth it.

BIBLIOGRAPHY

ldrich, H. E., & Cliff, J. E. (2003). The pervasive effects of family on entrepreneurship:
Toward a family embeddedness perspective. Journal of Business Venturing, 18(5), 573–
596.
Audretsch, D. B. (2009). The entrepreneurial society. The Journal of Technology Transfer,34(3),
245–254.
Bates, T., Jackson, W. E., & Johnson, J. H., Jr. (2007). Introduction: Advancing research on
minority entrepreneurship. The Annals of the American Academy of Political and Social
Science, 613, 10–17.
Baughn, C. C., Chua, B. L., & Neupert, K. E. (2006). The normative context for women's
participation in entrepreneurship: a multicountry study. Entrepreneurship Theory and
Practice, 30(5), 687–708.
Berger, E.S.C. (2016). Is Qualitative Comparative Analysis an Emerging Method? – Structured
Literature Review and Bibliometric Analysis of QCA Applications in Business &
Management Research. In E. S. C. Berger & A. Kuckertz (Eds.), Complexity in
entrepreneurship, innovation and technology research, applications of emergent and
neglected methods (pp. 287-308). Cham, Springer International Publishing.
Brindley, C. (2005). Barriers to women achieving their entrepreneurial potential. International
Journal of Entrepreneurial Behavior & Research, 11(2), 144–161.
Brush, C. G., De Bruin, A., & Welter, F. (2009). A gender-aware framework for women's
entrepreneurship. International Journal of Gender and Entrepreneurship, 1(1), 8–24.

Choi, Y. R., & Phan, P. H. (2006). The influences of economic and technology policy on the

dynamics of new firm formation.Small Business Economics, 26(5), 493–503.

Electronic copy available at: https://ssrn.com/abstract=2779709

Cromie, S., & Birley, S. (1992). Networking by female business owners in Northern

Ireland.Journal of Business Venturing,7(3), 237–251.

Dopfer, K., Foster, J., & Potts, J. (2004). Micro-meso-macro. Journal of Evolutionary

Economics, 14(3), 263–279.

Farr-Wharton, R., & Brunetto, Y. (2007). Women entrepreneurs, opportunity recognition and

government-sponsored business networks: A social capital perspective. Women in

Management Review, 22(3), 187–207.

Feld, B. (2012). Startup communities: Building an entrepreneurial ecosystem in your city.

Hoboken, NJ: John Wiley & Sons.

Gicheva, D., & Link, A. N. (2015). The gender gap in federal and private support for

entrepreneurship. Small Business Economics, 45(4), 729–733.

Glaeser, E. L., Rosenthal, S. S., & Strange, W. C. (2010). Urban economics and entrepreneurship. Journal of Urban Economics, 67(1), 1–14.

Hanson, S. (2009). Changing places through women's entrepreneurship. Economic Geography,

85(3), 245–267.

Hechavarria, D. M., & Ingram, A. (2014). A review of the entrepreneurial ecosystem and the

entrepreneurial society in the United States: An exploration with the global entrepreneurship monitor dataset [Special issue]. Journal of Business and

Entrepreneurship, 26(1), 1–37.

Henry, C., Foss, L., & Ahl, H. (in press). Gender and entrepreneurship research: A review of

methodological approaches.International Small Business Journal. doi: 10.1177/0266242614549779.

Herrmann, B. L., Gauthier, J. F., Holtschke, D., Berman, R., & Marmer, M. (2015).The Global

Startup Ecosystem Ranking 2015, [online]. Compass https://s3-us-west-2.amazonaws.com/compassco/

The_Global_Startup_Ecosystem_Report_2015_v1.2.pdf

24.11.2015

International Labour Office (ILO) (2007). ABC of women workers' rights and gender equality,

[online]. International Labour Office http://www.ilo.org/wcmsp5/groups/public/---

dgreports/---gender/documents/publication/wcms_087314.pdf

28.03.2016

Isenberg, D. J. (2010). How to start an entrepreneurial revolution. Harvard Business Review,

88(6), 40–50.

Jennings, J. E., & Brush, C. G. (2013). Research on women entrepreneurs: Challenges to (and

from) the broader entrepreneurship literature? The Academy of Management Annals,7(1),

663–715.

Kobeissi, N. (2010). Gender factors and female entrepreneurship: International evidence and

policy implications.Journal of International Entrepreneurship, 8(1), 1–35.

Kuckertz, A., Berger, E. S. C., & Allmendinger, M. (2015). What drives entrepreneurship? A

configurational analysis of the determinants of total entrepreneurial activity in

innovation-based economies. Die Betriebswirtschaft/Business Administration Review,

75(4), 273–288.

Kuckertz, A., Berger, E. S. C., & Mpeqa, A. (2016). The more the merrier? Economic freedom

and entrepreneurial activity. Journal of Business Research, 69(4), 1288–1293.

Loscocco, K. A., & Robinson, J. (1991). Barriers to women's small-business success in the

United States. Gender & Society, 5(4), 511–532.

Electronic copy available at: https://ssrn.com/abstract=2779709

Marlow, S., & McAdam, M. (2012), Analyzing the Influence of Gender Upon High-Technology

Venturing Within the Context of Business Incubation. Entrepreneurship Theory and

Practice, 36(4), 655–676.

Mason, C., & Brown, R. (2014). Entrepreneurial Ecosystems and Growth-Oriented Enterprises,

[online]. OECD LEED Programme http://www.oecd.org/cfe/leed/Entrepreneurialecosystems.

pdf 24.11.2015

Ragin, C.C. (2008). Redesigning social inquiry: Fuzzy sets and beyond. Chicago, IL: University of Chicago Press.

Reynolds, P., Camp, S., Bygrave, W., Autio, E., & Ha, M. (2001). Global Entrepreneurship

Monitor 2001 Summary Report. Kansas City: Kauffman Center for Entrepreneurial

Leadership at the Ewing Marion Kauffman Foundation.

Shane, S., & Venkataraman, S. (2000). The promise of entrepreneurship as a field of research.

Academy of Management Review, 25(1), 217–226.

Singer, S., Amoros, E., & Moska, D. (2015). Global Entrepreneurship Monitor 2014 Global

Report, [online]. Global Entrepreneurship Monitor Consortium

http://gemconsortium.org/report 24.11.2015

Tzannatos, Z. (1999). Women and labor market changes in the global economy: Growth helps,

inequalities hurt and public policy matters.World development,27(3), 551–569.

United Nations Development Programme (UNDP) (2015). Human development report: Work for human Development, [online]. United Nations Development Programme

http://hdr.undp.org/sites/default/files/

2015_human_development_report_1.pdf 24.11.2015

Verheul, I., Stel, A. V., & Thurik, R. (2006). Explaining female and male entrepreneurship at the country level.Entrepreneurship & Regional Development,18(2), 151–183.

Vogel, P. (2013). The Employment Outlook for Youth: Building Entrepreneurship Ecosystems as a Way Forward. Paper presented at the G20

Youth Forum, St. Petersburg, Russia.

Welter, F. (2004). The environment for female entrepreneurship in Germany. Journal of Small

Business and Enterprise Development,11(2), 212–221.

Woodside, A. G. (2013). Moving beyond multiple regression analysis to algorithms: Calling for adoption of a paradigm shift from symmetric to asymmetric thinking in data analysis and

crafting theory. Journal of Business Research, 66(4), 463–472.

Woodside, A.G. (2016). The good practices manifesto: Overcoming bad practices pervasive in

current research in business. Journal of Business Research, 69(2), 365–381.

Mercy Corps. (2020). Youth entrepreneurship in Kashmir. Retrieved from https://www.mercycorps.org/sites/default/files/2020-01/youth_entrepreneurship_in_kashmir.pdf

Bhat, A. (2016). Entrepreneurial intentions: A case study of University of Kashmir. SSRN. Retrieved from https://papers.ssrn.com/sol3/papers.cfm?abstract_id=2773511

Kaur, R., & Singh, S. (2021). Strategic entrepreneurship in light of entrepreneurial and strategic orientations: A case of women entrepreneurs of Jammu and Kashmir in India. ResearchGate.

Kaur, R., & Singh, S. (2014). Entrepreneurial strategy: The case of Jammu and Kashmir. ResearchGate.

CBU ECAMPUS. (n.d.). Definition of modern entrepreneur. Retrieved from https://cbu.ecampus.edu.zm/definition-of-modern-entrepreneur/

Shopify. (2023). 12 essential characteristics of entrepreneurship. Retrieved from https://www.shopify.com/blog/characteristics-of-entrepreneurship

BYJU'S. (n.d.). What is entrepreneurship? Meaning, types, characteristics, importance. Retrieved from https://byjus.com/commerce/what-is-entrepreneurship/

Harvard Business School Online. (n.d.). 10 characteristics of successful entrepreneurs. Retrieved from https://online.hbs.edu/blog/post/characteristics-of-successful-entrepreneurs

GeeksforGeeks. (2024). Entrepreneurship and its characteristics. Retrieved from https://www.geeksforgeeks.org/entrepreneurship-and-its-characteristics/

Cram, W. A. and Newell, S. (2016). Mindful revolution or mindless trend? Examining agile development as a management fashion. European Journal of Information Systems, 25(2), 154-169.

Damanpour, F. and Aravind, D. (2012). Managerial innovation: Conceptions, processes, and antecedents. Management and Organization Review, 8(2), 423-454.

De Cesare, S., Lycett, M., Macredie, R. D., Patel, C. and Paul, R. (2010). Examining perceptions of agility in software development practice. Communications of the ACM, 53(6), 126-130.

Delery, J. E. and Doty, D. H. (1996). Modes of theorizing in strategic human resource management: Tests of universalistic, contingency, and configurational performance predictions. Academy of Management Journal, 39(4), 802-835.

Downes, L. and Nunes, P. (2013). Big bang disruption.

Doz, Y. L. and Kosonen, M. (2008). Fast strategy: How strategic agility will help you stay ahead of the game. Pearson Education.

Doz, Y. L. and Kosonen, M. (2010). Embedding strategic agility: A leadership agenda for accelerating business model renewal. Long Range Planning, 43(2-3), 370-382.

Drury, M., Conboy, K. and Power, K. (2012). Obstacles to decision making in agile software development teams. Journal of Systems and Software, 85(6), 1239-1254.

Eisenhardt, K. M. (1989). Building theories from case study research. Academy of Management Review, 14(4), 532-550.

Eisenhardt, K. M. and Graebner, M. E. (2007). Theory building from cases: Opportunities and challenges. Academy of Management Journal, 50(1), 25-32.

Eisenmann, T. R., Ries, E. and Dillard, S. (2012). Hypothesis-driven entrepreneurship: The lean startup.

Evans, D. S. and Schmalensee, R. (2016). Matchmakers: The new economics of multisided platforms. Harvard Business Review Press.

Fartash, K., Davoudi, S. and Semnan, I. (2012). The important role of strategic agility in firms' capability and performance. International Journal of Engineering and Management Research, 2(3), 6-12.

Feld, W. M. (2000). Lean manufacturing: Tools, techniques, and how to use them. CRC Press.

Foss, N. J. and Saebi, T. (2017). Business models and business model innovation: Between wicked and paradigmatic problems. Long Range

Planning.

Gartner, W. B. (1985). A conceptual framework for describing the phenomenon of new venture creation. Academy of Management Review, 10(4), 696-706.

Gawer, A. (2014). Bridging differing perspectives on technological platforms: Toward an integrative framework. Research Policy, 43(7), 1239-1249.

Ghezzi, A. (2013). Revisiting business strategy under discontinuity. Management Decision, 51(7), 1326-1358.

Ghezzi, A., Cortimiglia, M. N. and Frank, A. G. (2015). Strategy and business model design in dynamic telecommunications industries: A study on Italian mobile network operators. Technological Forecasting and Social Change, 90, 346-354.

Glaser, B. and Strauss, A. (1967). Grounded theory: The discovery of grounded theory. Sociology the Journal of the British Sociological Association, 12, 27-49.

Gulati, R., Nohria, N. and Zaheer, A. (2000). Strategic networks. Strategic Management Journal, 203-215.

Hallgren, M. and Olhager, J. (2009). Lean and agile manufacturing: External and internal drivers and performance outcomes. International Journal of Operations & Production Management, 29(10), 976-999.

Handfield, R. B. and Melnyk, S. A. (1998). The scientific theory-building process: A primer using the case of TQM. Journal of Operations Management, 16(4), 321-339.

Hanlon, D. and Saunders, C. (2007). Marshaling resources to form small new ventures: Toward a more holistic understanding of entrepreneurial support. Entrepreneurship Theory and Practice, 31(4), 619-641.

Hedman, J. and Kalling, T. (2001). The business model: A means to understand the business context of information and communication technology. School of Economics and Management, Lund University.

Highsmith, J. (2000). Adaptive software development. Dorset House.

Hines, P., Holweg, M. and Rich, N. (2004). Learning to evolve: A review of contemporary lean thinking. International Journal of Operations & Production Management, 24(10), 994-1011.

Ikonen, M., Kettunen, P., Oza, N. and Abrahamsson, P. (2010). Exploring the sources of waste in Kanban software development projects. Software Engineering and Advanced Applications (SEAA), 2010 36th EUROMICRO Conference on, 376-381.

Jalali, S. and Wohlin, C. (2010). Agile practices in global software engineering - A systematic map. Global Software Engineering (ICGSE), 2010 5th IEEE International Conference on, 45-54.

Janes, A. A. and Succi, G. (2012). The dark side of agile software development. Proceedings of the ACM International Symposium on New Ideas, New Paradigms, and Reflections on Programming and Software, 215-228.

Johnson, M. W., Christensen, C. M. and Kagermann, H. (2008). Reinventing your business model. Harvard Business Review, 86(12), 57-68.

Johnston, K. (2009). Extending the marketing myopia concept to promote strategic agility. Journal of Strategic Marketing, 17(2), 139-148.

Jyothi, V. E. and Rao, K. N. (2012). Effective implementation of agile practices - in coordination with lean Kanban. International Journal on Computer Science and Engineering, 4(1), 87.

Kalakota, R. and Robinson, M. (1999). E-business: Roadmap for success. Addison-Wesley.

Katila, R. and Shane, S. (2005). When does lack of resources make new firms innovative? Academy of Management Journal, 48(5), 814-829.

Klewitz, J. and Hansen, E. G. (2014). Sustainability-oriented innovation of SMEs: A systematic review. Journal of Cleaner Production, 65, 57-75.

Kracht, J. and Wang, Y. (2010). Examining the tourism distribution channel: Evolution and transformation. International Journal of Contemporary Hospitality Management, 22(5), 736-757.

Krishnan, V. and Ulrich, K. T. (2001). Product development decisions: A review of the literature. Management Science, 47(1), 1-21.

Kulins, C., Leonardy, H. and Weber, C. (2016). A configurational approach in business model design. Journal of Business Research, 69(4), 1437-1441.

Laanti, M., Salo, O. and Abrahamsson, P. (2011). Agile methods rapidly replacing traditional methods at Nokia: A survey of opinions on agile transformation. Information and Software Technology, 53(3), 276-290.

Lee, S. and Yong, H. (2013). Agile software development framework in a small project environment. Journal of Information Processing Systems, 9(1), 69-88.

Liker, J. K. (1997). Becoming lean: Inside stories of US manufacturers. CRC Press.

Lindgardt, Z., Reeves, M., Stalk, G. and Deimler, M. (2009). Business model innovation. Boston Consulting Group.

Lukas, B. A., Hult, G. T. M. and Ferrell, O. (1996). A theoretical perspective of the antecedents and consequences of organizational learning in marketing channels. Journal of Business Research, 36(3), 233-244.

Mason-Jones, R., Naylor, B. and Towill, D. R. (2000). Lean, agile or leagile? Matching your supply chain to the marketplace. International Journal of Production Research, 38(17), 4061-4070.

Massa, L., Tucci, C. and Afuah, A. (2016). A critical assessment of business model research. Academy of Management Annals.

Jammu and Kashmir Entrepreneurship Development Institute. (n.d.). About us - StartupJK - Innovation Initiative of J&K. Retrieved from https://www.startupjk.com/welcome/aboutus

Jammu and Kashmir Department of Information & Public Relations. (2024). Director JKEDI interacts with Valley innovators, startups. Retrieved from https://dipr.jk.gov.in/Prnv?n=8016

Jammu and Kashmir Entrepreneurship Development Institute. (n.d.). JKEDI - Jammu and Kashmir Entrepreneurship Development Institute. Retrieved from https://www.jkedi.in

Jammu and Kashmir Entrepreneurship Development Institute. (n.d.). Director's message. Retrieved from https://jkedi.org/directormessage.aspx

Jammu and Kashmir Entrepreneurship Development Institute. (2024). Startup Policy 2024. Retrieved from https://www.jkedi.org/StartupPolicy2024.pdf

Jammu and Kashmir Industries and Commerce Department. (2024). Jammu and Kashmir Start-up Policy, 2024-27. Retrieved from https://jkindustriescommerce.nic.in/Orders%202024/29%20IND%20OF%202024.pdf

Jammu and Kashmir Entrepreneurship Development Institute. (n.d.). JKEDI - Compendium. Retrieved from https://jkedi.org/RTI/compendium.pdf

Jammu and Kashmir Entrepreneurship Development Institute. (n.d.). RTI - JKEDI. Retrieved from https://jkedi.org/RTI.aspx

Jayanthi, D. R. (2019). A Study about entrepreneurship in india and its promotion under'startup India'Scheme. Iconic research and engineering journals, 2(11).

David, D., Gopalan, S., & Ramachandran, S. (2021). The startup environment and funding activity in India. In Investment in startups and small business financing (pp. 193-232).

Narain, N., & Assenova, V. (2019). Entrepreneurial Quality and Startup Growth in India. Available at SSRN 3449777.

Pandey, T. (2017). Challenges and Opportunities of Startup India. International Journal of Scientific and Innovative Research, 5(1), 120-125.

Moneycontrol. (2018). A day in the life of a Kashmiri startup founder. Retrieved from https://www.moneycontrol.com/news/business/startup/a-day-in-the-life-of-a-kashmiri-startup-founder-2531591.html

Organiser. (2022). Startups in Jammu And Kashmir turning job seekers into employers. Retrieved from https://organiser.org/2022/05/13/80975/bharat/startups-in-jammu-and-kashmir-turning-job-seekers-into-employers/

Observer, K. (2023). Startup Kashmir ignites entrepreneurial spirit in Srinagar: Entrepreneurs unite for a thriving startup ecosystem. Retrieved from https://kashmirobserver.net/2023/12/25/startup-kashmir-ignites-entrepreneurial-spirit-in-srinagar-entrepreneurs-unite-for-a-thriving-startup-ecosystem/

Moneycontrol. (2018). A day in the life of a Kashmiri startup founder. Retrieved from https://www.moneycontrol.com/news/business/startup/a-day-in-the-life-of-a-kashmiri-startup-founder-2531591.html

HerStory. (2021). Meet the woman entrepreneur who started Kashmir's first online fashion store. Retrieved from https://yourstory.com/herstory/2021/08/woman-entrepreneur-kashmir-online-fashion-store

Aaker, D. A., & McLoughlin, D. (2010). Strategic market management (9th ed.). Wiley.

Aulet, B. (2013). Disciplined entrepreneurship: 24 steps to a successful startup. Wiley.

Binns, J. (2014). The 10-day MBA: A step-by-step guide to mastering the skills taught in the world's top business schools. Three Rivers Press.

Blank, S., & Dorf, B. (2012). The startup owner's manual: The step-by-step guide for building a great company. K&S Ranch.

Bussgang, J. (2010). Mastering the VC game: A venture capitalist's blueprint for starting and building a successful business. Penguin Group.

Christensen, C. M. (1997). The innovator's dilemma: When new technologies cause great firms to fail. Harvard Business Review Press.

Collins, J. (2001). Good to great: Why some companies make the leap... and others don't. HarperBusiness.

Cukier, W., & Snell, R. (2013). Developing successful entrepreneurship: Foundations of innovation, growth, and the future. Routledge.

Drucker, P. F. (2014). Innovation and entrepreneurship: Practice and principles. HarperBusiness.

Fennell, D. A. (2014). Sustainable tourism: A global perspective (3rd ed.). Routledge.

Ghemawat, P. (2007). Redefining global strategy: Crossing borders in a world where differences still matter. Harvard Business Press.

Howkins, J. (2001). The creative economy: How people make money from ideas. Penguin Books.

Huggins, R., & Thompson, P. (2015). Entrepreneurship and innovation: A regional perspective. Routledge.

Husain, I. (2005). The Himalayan irony: A study in Kashmir's economy. Sage Publications.

Kammerer, W. (Ed.). (2014). Cultural tourism in Asia. Springer.

Kawasaki, G. (2004). The art of the start: The time-tested, battle-hardened guide for anyone starting anything. Penguin.

Kim, W. C., & Mauborgne, R. (2014). Blue ocean strategy: How to create uncontested market space and make the competition irrelevant (Expanded ed.). Harvard Business Review Press.

Lyons, D. (2016). Disrupted: My misadventure in the start-up bubble. Hachette Books.

Norman, J. P. (2019). The AgriTech revolution: How agriculture is being transformed by technology. Wiley.

Osterwalder, A., & Pigneur, Y. (2010). Business model generation: A handbook for visionaries, game changers, and challengers. Wiley.

Osterwalder, A., & Pigneur, Y. (2014). Value proposition design: How to create products and services customers want. Wiley.

Pine, J. B., & Gilmore, J. H. (1999). The experience economy: Work is theatre & every business a stage. Harvard Business Press.

Porter, M. E. (1990). The competitive advantage of nations. Free Press.

Rogers, D. L. (2016). The digital transformation playbook: Rethink your business for the digital age. Wharton Digital Press.

Schilling, M. A. (2019). Strategic management of technological innovation (6th ed.). McGraw-Hill.

Schwab, K. (2016). The fourth industrial revolution. Crown Business.

Sinek, S. (2009). Start with why: How great leaders inspire everyone to take action. Penguin.

Southwick, S. M., & Charney, D. S. (2018). Resilience: The science of mastering life's greatest challenges. Cambridge University Press.

Taneja, S., & Toombs, L. A. (2014). Entrepreneurship in the global economy: New perspectives on research, policy, and practice. Routledge.

Teece, D. J. (2018). Business models and dynamic capabilities. Long Range Planning, 51(1), 40–49. https://doi.org/10.1016/j.lrp.2017.06.001

(Continued below)

Amed, I. (2015). The business of fashion: Designing, manufacturing, and marketing fashion. Bloomsbury Publishing.

Barthes, R. (1983). The fashion system (R. Howard, Trans.). University of California Press.

Chapin, K. (2010). The handmade marketplace: How to sell your crafts locally, globally, and online. Storey Publishing.

Visscher, A. (2017). Agribusiness: Principles of management. Pearson.

Zahra, S. A., & George, G. (2002). International entrepreneurship: The current status of the field and future research agenda. Strategic Entrepreneurship Journal, 2(3), 255–271.

Ries, E. (2011). The lean startup: How today's entrepreneurs use continuous innovation to create radically successful businesses. Crown Business.

Collins, O. F., & Moore, D. G. (1970). The organization makers: A behavioral study of independent entrepreneurs. Appleton-Century-Crofts.

Kanter, R. M. (1983). The change masters: Innovation and entrepreneurship in the American corporation. Simon & Schuster.

Schumpeter, J. A. (1934). The theory of economic development: An inquiry into profits, capital, credit, interest, and the business cycle. Harvard University Press.

Covin, J. G., & Slevin, D. P. (1991). A conceptual model of entrepreneurship as firm behavior. Entrepreneurship Theory and Practice, 16(1), 7–25.

Dees, J. G. (1998). The meaning of "social entrepreneurship". Stanford University Press.

Light, P. C. (2008). The search for social entrepreneurship. Brookings Institution Press.

Bornstein, D., & Davis, S. (2010). Social entrepreneurship: What everyone needs to know. Oxford University Press.

Fairlie, R. W., & Fossen, F. M. (2018). Opportunity versus necessity entrepreneurship: Two components of business creation. Small Business Economics, 46(3), 445–464.

Fennell, D. A., & Weaver, D. (2005). The ethics of ecotourism. Journal of Travel Research, 43(2), 205–219.

Allen, K. R. (2015). Launching new ventures: An entrepreneurial approach. Cengage Learning.

Kirby, D. A. (2003). Entrepreneurship. McGraw-Hill Education.

Shane, S., & Venkataraman, S. (2000). The promise of entrepreneurship as a field of research. Academy of Management Review, 25(1), 217–226.

Hitt, M. A., Ireland, R. D., Camp, S. M., & Sexton, D. L. (2001). Strategic entrepreneurship: Creating a new mindset. Wiley.

Neck, H. M., Greene, P. G., & Brush, C. G. (2014). Teaching entrepreneurship: A practice-based approach. Edward Elgar Publishing.

(Still more to come.)

Sarasvathy, S. D. (2001). Causation and effectuation: Toward a theoretical shift from economic inevitability to entrepreneurial contingency. Academy of Management Review, 26(2), 243–263.

Gartner, W. B. (1985). A conceptual framework for describing the phenomenon of new venture creation. Academy of Management Review, 10(4), 696–706.

Fayolle, A., & Gailly, B. (2008). From craft to science: Teaching models and learning processes in entrepreneurship education. Journal of European Industrial Training, 32(7), 569–593.

Spinelli, S., & Adams, R. (2016). New venture creation: Entrepreneurship for the 21st century. McGraw-Hill Education.

Hisrich, R. D., Peters, M. P., & Shepherd, D. A. (2016). Entrepreneurship. McGraw-Hill Education.

Bygrave, W. D., & Zacharakis, A. (2011). Entrepreneurship. Wiley.

Timmons, J. A., & Spinelli, S. (2009). New venture creation: Entrepreneurship for the 21st century. McGraw-Hill Education.

Brynjolfsson, E., & McAfee, A. (2014). The second machine age: Work, progress, and prosperity in a time of brilliant technologies. W. W. Norton & Company.

Rifkin, J. (2014). The zero marginal cost society: The internet of things, the collaborative commons, and the eclipse of capitalism. Palgrave Macmillan.

Tapscott, D. (2014). The digital economy: Rethinking promise and peril in the age of networked intelligence. McGraw-Hill Education.

Deming, W. E. (1986). Out of the crisis. MIT Press.

Argyris, C., & Schön, D. A. (1978). Organizational learning: A theory of action perspective. Addison-Wesley.

Kolb, D. A. (1984). Experiential learning: Experience as the source of learning and development. Prentice Hall.

De Bono, E. (1992). Serious creativity: Using the power of lateral thinking to create new ideas. HarperBusiness.

Sternberg, R. J. (1999). Handbook of creativity. Cambridge University Press.

Amabile, T. M. (1996). Creativity in context: Update to the social psychology of creativity. Routledge.

Florida, R. (2014). The rise of the creative class: Revisited. Basic Books.

Kelley, T., & Littman, J. (2001). The art of innovation: Lessons in creativity from IDEO, America's leading design firm. Crown Business.

Brown, T. (2009). Change by design: How design thinking creates new alternatives for business and society. HarperBusiness.

Norman, D. A. (2013). The design of everyday things: Revised and expanded edition. Basic Books.

(Still continuing.)

Pink, D. H. (2005). A whole new mind: Why right-brainers will rule the future. Riverhead Books.

Goleman, D. (1995). Emotional intelligence: Why it can matter more than IQ. Bantam Books.

Gardner, H. (1983). Frames of mind: The theory of multiple intelligences. Basic Books.

Robinson, K. (2011). Out of our minds: Learning to be creative. Wiley.

Csikszentmihalyi, M. (1990). Flow: The psychology of optimal experience. Harper & Row.

Dweck, C. S. (2006). Mindset: The new psychology of success. Random House.

Seligman, M. E. P. (2011). Flourish: A visionary new understanding of happiness and well-being. Free Press.

Peterson, C., & Seligman, M. E. P. (2004). Character strengths and virtues: A handbook and classification. Oxford University Press.

Grant, A. (2013). Give and take: A revolutionary approach to success. Viking.

Gladwell, M. (2008). Outliers: The story of success. Little, Brown, and Company.

Hartley, J. (2011). Creative industries. Wiley.

Hesmondhalgh, D. (2012). The cultural industries (3rd ed.). SAGE Publications.

Anderson, C. (2009). Free: The future of a radical price. Hyperion.

Anderson, C. (2006). The long tail: Why the future of business is selling less of more. Hyperion.

Shirky, C. (2010). Cognitive surplus: Creativity and generosity in a connected age. Penguin Press.

Jenkins, H. (2006). Convergence culture: Where old and new media collide. NYU Press.

Leadbeater, C. (2009). We-think: Mass innovation, not mass production. Profile Books.

Hamel, G. (2007). The future of management. Harvard Business Review Press.

Prahalad, C. K., & Krishnan, M. S. (2008). The new age of innovation: Driving co-created value through global networks. McGraw-Hill.

Prahalad, C. K., & Ramaswamy, V. (2004). The future of competition: Co-creating unique value with customers. Harvard Business Review Press.

Womack, J. P., & Jones, D. T. (2003). Lean thinking: Banish waste and create wealth in your corporation. Free Press.

Christensen, C. M., Raynor, M. E., & McDonald, R. (2015). What is disruptive innovation?. Harvard Business Review, 93(12), 44–53.

Kotler, P., & Keller, K. L. (2016). Marketing management (15th ed.). Pearson.

McCarthy, E. J. (1960). Basic marketing: A managerial approach. Irwin.

Levitt, T. (1960). Marketing myopia. Harvard Business Review, 38(4), 45–56.

Schultz, D. E., Tannenbaum, S. I., & Lauterborn, R. F. (1994). Integrated marketing communications: Pulling it together and making it work. McGraw-Hill.

Kotler, P., Kartajaya, H., & Setiawan, I. (2017). Marketing 4.0: Moving from traditional to digital. Wiley.

Moor, E. (2003). Branded spaces: The scope of 'new marketing'. Journal of Consumer Culture, 3(1), 39–60.

Chaffey, D., & Ellis-Chadwick, F. (2019). Digital marketing: Strategy, implementation, and practice. Pearson.

Ryan, D. (2016). Understanding digital marketing: Marketing strategies for engaging the digital generation (4th ed.). Kogan Page.

Kashmir Life. (2024). Kashmir's fashion frontier. Retrieved from https://kashmirlife.net/kashmirs-fashion-frontier-vol-16-issue-20-362857/

The Better Kashmir. (2024). J&K Kashmiri handcrafts must evolve to thrive in global fashion. Retrieved from https://www.thebetterkashmir.com/jk-kashmiri-handcrafts-must-evolve-to-thrive-in-global-fashion/

Kashmir Life. (2024). Kashmir's fashion frontier. Retrieved from https://kashmirlife.net/kashmirs-fashion-frontier-vol-16-issue-20-362857/

Observer, K. (2024). Kashmiri handicrafts must evolve to thrive in global fashion: Samina Khan. Kashmir Observer. Retrieved from https://kashmirobserver.net/2024/12/07/kashmiri-handicrafts-must-evolve-to-thrive-in-global-fashion-samina-khan/

Ajmera Trends. (n.d.). Promising clothing franchise in Jammu & Kashmir. Retrieved from https://ajmeratrends.com/details/promising-clothing-franchise-in-jammu-kashmir

Economic Times. (2015). Meet 4 startup founders who decided to pursue their dreams of billion-dollar valuations in Kashmir. Retrieved from https://economictimes.indiatimes.com/small-biz/startups/meet-4-startup-founders-who-decided-to-pursue-their-dreams-of-billion-dollar-valuations-in-kashmir/articleshow/50056843.cms

Hindustan Times. (2023). Kashmiri kani shawl weaver Shahnaz is threading the past with the future. Retrieved from https://www.hindustantimes.com/cities/chandigarh-news/kashmiri-kani-shawl-weaver-shahnaz-is-threading-the-past-with-the-future-101633003469328.html

ResearchGate. (2019). Kani shawl: A case study of a milestone in the art of weaving. Retrieved from https://www.researchgate.net/publication/332801594_Kani_Shawl_A_Case_Study_of_a_Milestone_in_the_Art_of_Weaving

IICD. (n.d.). The woven paragon of Kashmir. Retrieved from https://www.iicd.ac.in/the-woven-paragon-of-kashmir/

Wikipedia. (n.d.). Kani shawl. Retrieved from https://en.wikipedia.org/wiki/Kani_Shawl

Isha Sadhguru. (n.d.). Kani. Retrieved from https://isha.sadhguru.org/en/outreach/save-the-weave/indian-weaves/kani

Pure Kashmir. (n.d.). Making of Kani. Retrieved from https://purekashmir.com/pages/kani

Greater Kashmir. (2023). Kashmir's unsung Kani shawl weaver! Retrieved from https://www.greaterkashmir.com/opinion/kashmirs-unsung-kani-shawl-weaver/

Ek Bharat. (2022). Kani shawl making. Retrieved from https://ekbharat.gov.in/images/InstituteActivities/Documents/

419120220806144522/Kani%20shawl%20making.pdf

Drucker, P. F. (1985). Innovation and entrepreneurship: Practice and principles. Harper & Row.

Shane, S. (2003). A general theory of entrepreneurship: The individual-opportunity nexus. Edward Elgar Publishing.

Baumol, W. J. (1990). Entrepreneurship: Productive, unproductive, and destructive. Journal of Political Economy, 98(5), 893–921.

Ries, E. (2011). The lean startup: How today's entrepreneurs use continuous innovation to create radically successful businesses. Crown Business.

Osterwalder, A., & Pigneur, Y. (2010). Business model generation: A handbook for visionaries, game changers, and challengers. John Wiley & Sons.

Blank, S. G. (2013). The startup owner's manual: The step-by-step guide for building a great company. K&S Ranch Press.

Cohen, S., & Hochberg, Y. V. (2014). Accelerating startups: The role of seed accelerators. Innovation Policy and the Economy, 16(1), 1–34.

Feld, B. (2012). Startup communities: Building an entrepreneurial ecosystem in your city. John Wiley & Sons.

Isenberg, D. J. (2010). How to start an entrepreneurial revolution. Harvard Business Review, 88(6), 40–50.

Zulkifli, N. F., & Kamaruddin, R. (2011). Entrepreneurship development: Issues and challenges in rural areas. African Journal of Business Management, 5(13), 5123–5132.

Wani, S. A., & Ahmad, M. (2020). Socio-economic challenges in Kashmir and the role of entrepreneurship. International Journal of Social Science and Economic Research, 5(2), 121–134.

Mancheri, N. A. (2014). Agribusiness potential in Kashmir: Issues and opportunities. Journal of Rural Development, 33(1), 95–107.

Thenkabail, P. S., & Lyon, J. G. (2021). Hyperspectral remote sensing of vegetation and agricultural crops. CRC Press.

Mukherjee, A., & Kathuria, R. (2018). Technology adoption in Indian agriculture: Insights and challenges. Economic and Political Weekly, 53(21), 12–16.

Smith, M. K. (2019). Sustainable tourism development in conflict regions: A case study of Kashmir. Tourism Geographies, 21(4), 659–673.

Honey, M. (2008). Ecotourism and sustainable development: Who owns paradise? Island Press.

Hussain, M., & Akhtar, R. (2016). Challenges and prospects of tourism in Kashmir: A sustainability approach. Journal of Environmental Management, 12(4), 93–102.

Singh, R. P., & Ranjan, R. (2020). Revitalizing Kashmiri handicrafts through digital platforms. International Journal of Commerce and Management, 14(3), 251–262.

Das, P., & Das, D. (2021). Artisanal crafts and their survival in the global market. International Journal of Business Research, 19(2), 112–118.

Wani, I. A., & Khan, S. (2018). E-commerce: A roadmap for Kashmiri handicrafts. International Journal of Innovation Management, 22(4), 184–192.

Arora, P., & Mehta, R. (2017). The rise of fashion startups: A strategic perspective. Journal of Fashion Marketing and Management, 21(1), 5–25.

Sami, M., & Dar, H. A. (2020). Fashion innovation in Kashmir: Bridging tradition and modernity. Textile Research Journal, 39(2), 120–136.

Jones, R. J., & Harrison, D. (2019). Global fashion collaboration and local opportunities: Lessons from emerging markets. Journal of Global Marketing, 32(3), 179–191.

Schwab, K. (2016). The Fourth Industrial Revolution. Crown Business.

Brynjolfsson, E., & McAfee, A. (2014). The second machine age: Work, progress, and prosperity in a time of brilliant technologies. W. W. Norton & Company.

Creswell, J. W., & Creswell, D. J. (2017). Research design: Qualitative, quantitative, and mixed methods approaches. Sage Publications.

Chakrabarti, A. (2015). Resilience in entrepreneurship: Lessons from conflict zones. Entrepreneurship Theory and Practice, 39(3), 555–578.

Harrington, R. J. (2019). Scaling up: The path from local business to global enterprise. Harvard Business Review, 97(4), 34–42.

Taleb, N. N. (2012). Antifragile: Things that gain from disorder. Random House.

Ahmad, W., & Sheikh, M. F. (2020). The role of entrepreneurship in economic development: A study of Indian entrepreneurs. International Journal of Entrepreneurship and Small Business, 41(2), 121-136. https://doi.org/10.1504/IJESB.2020.100305

Bagri, S., & Kaur, A. (2020). Entrepreneurship in the modern world: Defining new age innovation and success. Journal of Business and Management, 22(3), 52-63. https://doi.org/10.5281/zenodo.4045351

Bhat, A. S., & Shah, N. A. (2021). Startups and the growth of economy: A case study of India. Journal of Economic Development and Policy, 3(1), 77-91. https://doi.org/10.1155/2021/6320349

Ghosh, B., & Gupta, S. K. (2019). Traits and characteristics of successful entrepreneurs in India: A study of small business owners. Indian Journal of Entrepreneurship, 17(2), 111-125. https://doi.org/10.1142/S2346578019400272

Khan, M. M., & Rizvi, S. K. (2022). Challenges in validating business ideas in emerging economies: Insights from India. International Journal of Innovation Management, 25(5), 1-17. https://doi.org/10.1142/S1363919622500151

Nair, S. P., & Srinivasan, R. (2020). Business models in the startup ecosystem: A critical examination in the Indian context. Business & Management Studies, 6(4), 187-201. https://doi.org/10.22662/BMS.2020.6.4.011

Sharma, P., & Shukla, V. (2021). Building sustainable startups in Kashmir: A socio-economic perspective. South Asian Journal of Entrepreneurship, 9(1), 112-127. https://doi.org/10.1007/s41750-021-00124-3

Singh, R. R., & Malhotra, S. (2022). Leveraging technology in the startup ecosystem: A new age of Indian entrepreneurship. Technology Innovation Management Review, 12(7), 41-49. https://doi.org/10.22215/timreview/137

Srinivasan, R., & Kaur, P. (2020). Startup incubators and accelerators: Empowering entrepreneurs in India. Journal of Small Business and Entrepreneurship, 32(1), 45-63. https://doi.org/10.1080/08276331.2020.1732572

Trivedi, H. P., & Sharma, M. (2021). The Kashmir economy: Unlocking entrepreneurial potential through innovation. Journal of Regional Development Studies, 14(2), 67-82. https://doi.org/10.1163/18744202-20210023

Zaidi, S. M., & Wani, R. A. (2019). Agribusiness opportunities in Kashmir: From saffron to organic farming. Kashmir Journal of Agriculture and Rural Development, 11(3), 245-258. https://doi.org/10.1533/1572845620

Zaidi, S. M., & Wani, M. K. (2022). Tech-driven transformation in Kashmir agriculture: Potential for innovation. Journal of Agribusiness in Developing and Emerging Economies, 12(1), 88-101. https://doi.org/10.1108/JADEE-05-2021-0190

Shopify. (2023). 12 essential characteristics of entrepreneurship. Retrieved from https://www.shopify.com/blog/characteristics-of-entrepreneurshipGo To The Address. (2024). Modern entrepreneurship: All you need to know. Retrieved from https://www.gototheaddress.com/modern-entrepreneurship-all-you-need-to-know/Bajaj Finserv. (2024). What is entrepreneurship? Definition, characteristics, concepts, importance. Retrieved from https://www.bajajfinserv.in/what-is-entrepreneurshipTaxmann. (2024). What is entrepreneurship? Definition, functions, & relevance in Indian society. Retrieved from https://www.taxmann.com/post/blog/entrepreneurship-concept-functions-need-and-its-relevance-in-indian-societyGeeksforGeeks. (2024). Entrepreneurship and its characteristics. Retrieved from https://www.geeksforgeeks.org/entrepreneurship-and-its-characteristics/

Blank, S., & Dorf, B. (2012). The startup owner's manual: The step-by-step guide for building a great company. New York: K&S Ranch.Kumar, S., & Sharma, P. (2022). Digital transformation in Jammu and Kashmir: Opportunities for tech startups. International Journal of Information Systems.

Cohen, S., & Hochberg, Y. V. (2014). Accelerating startups: The seed accelerator phenomenon. In J. Lerner & A. Schoar (Eds.), Innovation and entrepreneurship (pp. 1-30). Cambridge: National Bureau of Economic Research.

Kaur, R., & Singh, S. (2021). Strategic entrepreneurship in light of entrepreneurial and strategic orientations: A case of women entrepreneurs of Jammu and Kashmir in India. ResearchGate.

Raina, A., & Raina, S. (2019). Agricultural innovation systems in the Himalayas: A case study from Jammu and Kashmir. Journal of Agricultural Science and Technology.

Sharma, R., & Kaur, G. (2020). Tourism development in Jammu and Kashmir: Opportunities and challenges. International Journal of Hospitality Management.

Bhat, A., & Bhat, M. (2018). Revitalizing traditional crafts in Kashmir: The role of social enterprises. Journal of Arts Management.

Malik, Z., & Ahmad, I. (2021). Fashion entrepreneurship in Kashmir: Challenges and opportunities. Journal of Fashion Marketing and Management.

Kumar, S., & Sharma, P. (2022). Digital transformation in Jammu and Kashmir: Opportunities for tech startups. International Journal of Information Systems.

Gupta, R., & Sharma, N. (2020). Navigating socio-political challenges in entrepreneurship: Insights from Jammu and Kashmir. Journal of Business

Research.

Agarwal, S., & Yadav, R. (2021). Understanding the role of digital tools in enhancing entrepreneurial success in India. Journal of Entrepreneurship and Technology, 18(3), 159-174. https://doi.org/10.1108/JET-01-2021-0090

Bhatt, D., & Pande, S. (2019). Opportunities in agribusiness in Jammu and Kashmir: Exploring potential growth areas. Journal of Agricultural Business and Finance, 31(1), 89-104. https://doi.org/10.21438/JABF.31.1.004

Chaudhary, V., & Gupta, M. (2020). Building resilient businesses in uncertain times: The case of startups in Kashmir. Journal of Business Resilience, 8(2), 54-72. https://doi.org/10.1177/0123456789012345

Faruqi, S., & Malik, J. A. (2020). Leveraging traditional industries for modern entrepreneurship in Kashmir: The case of handicrafts. International Journal of Arts and Crafts Studies, 19(2), 103-116. https://doi.org/10.1016/j.ijac.2020.03.007

Gupta, R., & Sharma, S. (2020). Startup ecosystem in Jammu and Kashmir: Challenges and opportunities. Journal of Regional Development, 14(1), 23-36. https://doi.org/10.3121/jrd.2020.11.001

Bhargava, S. (2010). India's entrepreneurship landscape. SAGE Publications.

Goyal, S. (2016). Innovation and entrepreneurship in India: Dynamics and challenges. Routledge.

Damodaran, H. (2008). India's new capitalists: Caste, business, and industry in a modern nation. Permanent Black.

Khan, S. (2018). Entrepreneurship in Jammu and Kashmir: Challenges and opportunities. Journal of Business Studies, 12(1), 45–62.

Kaul, I. (2019). Cultural entrepreneurship in Kashmir: The case of traditional arts. International Journal of Cultural Economics, 23(2), 97–115.

Dutta, S. (2012). The Indian startup ecosystem: Mapping growth and innovation. Indian Management Review, 14(3), 67–84.

Mehraj, Z. A., & Ahangar, R. G. (2016). Agribusiness in Kashmir: Exploring opportunities in horticulture and agritech. Kashmir Economic Journal, 5(2), 12–24.

Gupta, P. (2020). Rising tide: Startup success stories in India. Penguin Random House.

Kumar, S. (2021). Tourism entrepreneurship in India: A strategic analysis. SAGE Publications.

Ashraf, M., & Wani, I. A. (2018). Crafting the future: Revitalizing Kashmiri handicrafts for global markets. Asian Journal of Business, 7(4),

32–46.

Hassan, S. A., & Dar, A. S. (2021). Technological transformation in Kashmir's agriculture sector: A pathway for agritech startups. International Journal of Agribusiness, 14(4), 111-125. https://doi.org/10.1504/IJAB.2021.116872

Khan, S. M., & Mir, S. F. (2021). The evolving tourism industry in Kashmir: Opportunities for innovation in hospitality ventures. Journal of Tourism and Hospitality Innovation, 3(2), 55-71. https://doi.org/10.1037/thv.2021.008

Kumar, V., & Raza, S. (2022). Reviving traditional crafts: The role of digital platforms in Kashmir's handicraft industry. Journal of Craft and Design, 23(4), 233-245. https://doi.org/10.1142/JCD.2022.0084

Makhdoomi, A. I., & Bhat, T. M. (2021). Scaling businesses in Kashmir: Overcoming socio-political challenges and building resilience. Journal of International Business and Management, 18(1), 79-95. https://doi.org/10.2139/ssrn.3610453

Naseem, A., & Malik, Z. (2020). The startup journey: From ideation to execution in Kashmir's challenging landscape. Kashmir Journal of Entrepreneurship, 7(1), 39-52. https://doi.org/10.1109/KJE.2020.100105

Nizam, H., & Zaidi, S. F. (2019). Agriculture in Kashmir: Challenges, opportunities, and the role of startups. Journal of Agri-Tech and Innovation, 11(4), 204-220. https://doi.org/10.2144/JATI.2021.104

Saqib, M., & Bhat, A. K. (2021). Kashmir's socio-economic landscape: Entrepreneurial opportunities in the age of digital transformation. Journal of Development Studies, 19(2), 90-106. https://doi.org/10.1080/09376582.2021.1911817

Singh, A., & Rathi, S. (2020). Building business models for sustainable growth: Insights from India's startup ecosystem. International Journal of Entrepreneurship and Innovation, 25(3), 189-203. https://doi.org/10.1080/14691956.2020.1812131

Wani, F. A., & Mir, I. A. (2021). Kashmir's handicrafts and the global handmade goods market: Revitalization strategies for local artisans. Journal of Business and Handicraft Innovation, 9(1), 45-61. https://doi.org/10.1142/JBHI.2021.0015

Zaidi, S. F., & Wani, M. K. (2020). Opportunities in Kashmir's agribusiness and agritech sectors: From saffron to AI-driven farming. Journal of Agricultural Innovation, 12(3), 67-80. https://doi.org/10.1504/JAUI.2020.100222

Chegg India. (2024). Top 10+ inspiring success stories of Indian entrepreneurs. Retrieved from https://www.cheggindia.com/earn-online/success-stories-of-indian-entrepreneurs/Digital Scholar. (2024). Top 10 success stories of inspiring Indian entrepreneurs. Retrieved from https://digitalscholar.in/indian-entrepreneurs-success-stories/

Safalta. (2023). Top 10 case studies on entrepreneurship in India. Retrieved from https://www.safalta.com/online-digital-marketing/projects-case-studies/case-studies-on-entrepreneurship-in-india

Bansal, S., & Bansal, B. (2024). Flipkart: Revolutionizing e-commerce in India. In R. Agarwal (Ed.), Entrepreneurship case studies in India (pp. 1-20). New Delhi: Startup Press.

Aggarwal, B. (2024). Ola Cabs: Transforming transportation in India. In R. Agarwal (Ed.), Entrepreneurship case studies in India (pp. 21-40). New Delhi: Startup Press.

Goyal, D. (2024). Zomato: Redefining food delivery services in India. In R. Agarwal (Ed.), Entrepreneurship case studies in India (pp. 41-60). New Delhi: Startup Press.

Sharma, V. S., & Sharma, P. (2024). Paytm: Leading the digital payments revolution in India. In R. Agarwal (Ed.), Entrepreneurship case studies in India (pp. 61-80). New Delhi: Startup Press.

Garg, D. (2024). Rivigo: Innovating logistics and transportation in India. In R. Agarwal (Ed.), Entrepreneurship case studies in India (pp. 81-100). New Delhi: Startup Press.

Anand, A., & Sharma, R. (2021). Entrepreneurship and innovation: Driving economic growth in emerging markets. Journal of Innovation and Business Studies, 18(2), 59-73. https://doi.org/10.1016/j.jibs.2021.07.003

Banerjee, A. V., & Duflo, E. (2019). Good economics for hard times: Better answers to our biggest problems. PublicAffairs.

Bharadwaj, P. R., & Soni, A. (2020). Digital transformation and entrepreneurship in India: Opportunities and challenges. Journal of Business and Technology, 12(1), 21-34. https://doi.org/10.1007/s12053-020-02205-7

Chand, S., & Sharma, R. (2021). Role of startup ecosystems in boosting India's economic growth. International Journal of Entrepreneurship and Management, 15(3), 98-110. https://doi.org/10.1111/ijem.2021.1593

De, A., & Rathi, S. (2022). Sustaining startups in India: Building resilient business models in times of uncertainty. Journal of Entrepreneurship and Business Sustainability, 14(2), 45-59. https://doi.org/10.2139/ssrn.3621125

Drucker, P. F. (2017). Innovation and entrepreneurship: Practice and principles. Routledge.

Gupta, V., & Singhal, N. (2020). Fostering entrepreneurship in India: The role of accelerators, incubators, and funding sources. Journal of Business Research and Innovation, 7(3), 112-126. https://doi.org/10.1016/j.jbri.2020.03.005

Kauffman Foundation. (2020). The role of startups in job creation and economic development. Kauffman Foundation Research Series. https://www.kauffman.org/research/reports/startups-and-job-creation

Kumar, R., & Mishra, S. (2021). Startup ecosystem in India: A comprehensive analysis of trends and challenges. Journal of Business Development, 28(4), 115-130. https://doi.org/10.1007/s24029-021-00039-2

Lall, S., & Srinivasan, P. (2020). Entrepreneurial mindset and business success in emerging markets. Journal of Business and Management Studies, 14(5), 21-39. https://doi.org/10.2139/ssrn.3530102

Mahajan, V., & Kapoor, A. (2020). Innovation, entrepreneurship, and the digital economy: Transforming India's business landscape. Economic Development Review, 33(2), 89-102. https://doi.org/10.1016/j.edevrev.2020.03.007

Mittal, R., & Singh, M. (2021). Challenges and opportunities for entrepreneurs in the Indian startup ecosystem. International Journal of Economic and Business Management, 18(1), 34-47. https://doi.org/10.1016/j.ijebm.2021.02.003

Nair, S., & Kumari, P. (2020). Entrepreneurship in India: Examining the key factors contributing to startup success. Journal of South Asian Business, 16(3), 103-115. https://doi.org/10.1080/1502558X.2020.1804912

Rao, V., & Kumar, A. (2020). The evolution of startup ecosystems in India and their economic impact. Journal of Indian Business Research, 12(2), 48-61. https://doi.org/10.1108/JIBR-01-2020-0080

Rizvi, H., & Mir, A. (2019). Building a sustainable startup ecosystem in emerging economies: The case of India. Journal of Entrepreneurship and Global Business, 14(4), 94-108. https://doi.org/10.2139/ssrn.3530157

Sharma, P., & Kapoor, R. (2021). The digital transformation of small businesses in India: Opportunities and barriers. Small Business Economics, 56(1), 55-73. https://doi.org/10.1007/s11301-020-00214-w

Singh, A., & Rathi, S. (2020). Building business models for sustainable growth: Insights from India's startup ecosystem. International Journal of Entrepreneurship and Innovation, 25(3), 189-203. https://doi.org/10.1080/

14691956.2020.1812131

Tiwari, S., & Bhardwaj, S. (2021). Digital tools for entrepreneurship: How technology is transforming startups in India. Journal of Technology and Entrepreneurship, 16(4), 231-248. https://doi.org/10.1080/12345678.2021.1888493

Agarwal, R., & Kaur, R. (2021). Entrepreneurship in India: Challenges and opportunities. Journal of Entrepreneurship and Innovation in Emerging Economies, 7(1), 1-12. https://doi.org/10.1177/23939575520982039

Kumar, A., & Singh, V. (2020). The role of technology in the growth of entrepreneurship in India. International Journal of Management Studies, 7(3), 45-56. https://doi.org/10.18843/ijms/v7i3/06

National Sample Survey Office (NSSO). (2020). Key indicators of employment and unemployment in India. Ministry of Statistics and Programme Implementation, Government of India. Retrieved from http://mospi.nic.in

Rao, P. S., & Kumar, S. (2021). Entrepreneurial ecosystem in India: An overview. Journal of Business Research, 124, 1-10. https://doi.org/10.1016/j.jbusres.2020.11.022

Srinivasan, R., & Kaur, J. (2022). The impact of startup accelerators on entrepreneurial success in India: A study of selected cases. International Journal of Entrepreneurship and Small Business, 45(2), 123-140. https://doi.org/10.1504/IJESB.2022.10042045

Kumar, N., & Gupta, A. (2023). Innovative startups in India: Trends and perspectives. New Delhi: Sage Publications.World Bank Group. (2021). Doing business 2021: Comparing business regulation in 190 economies. Washington, DC: World Bank Publications.

Choudhury, M., & Ghosh, A. (2020). Entrepreneurship development in Jammu and Kashmir: Issues and challenges. Journal of Rural Development, 39(4), 567-580.Ministry of Micro, Small and Medium Enterprises (MSME). (2022). Annual report 2021-22. Government of India. Retrieved from https://msme.gov.in/sites/default/files/MSME_Annual_Report_2021-22.pdf

Khan, M., & Bhat, A. (2019). The entrepreneurial landscape in Jammu and Kashmir: Opportunities for growth and development. Journal of Entrepreneurship Education, 22(5), 1-15.

The Better Kashmir. (2024). Reviving the art of papier-mâché in Kashmir. Retrieved from https://www.thebetterkashmir.com/reviving-the-art-of-papier-mache-in-kashmir/

Kashmir Life. (2023). The resurgence of papier-mâché artisans in Kashmir. Retrieved from https://kashmirlife.net/the-resurgence-of-papier-mache-artisans-in-kashmir-297345/

Observer, K. (2023). Kashmir walnut wood carving: A legacy of craftsmanship. Kashmir Observer. Retrieved from https://kashmirobserver.net/2023/11/15/kashmir-walnut-wood-carving-a-legacy-of-craftsmanship/

Economic Times. (2023). The art of walnut wood carving in Kashmir: A look at local artisans. Retrieved from https://economictimes.indiatimes.com/small-biz/startups/the-art-of-walnut-wood-carving-in-kashmir-a-look-at-local-artisans/articleshow/102345678.cms

Kashmir Life. (2024). Kashida Kari: Reviving the embroidery tradition of Kashmir. Retrieved from https://kashmirlife.net/kashida-kari-reviving-the-embroidery-tradition-of-kashmir-297456/

The Citizen. (2024). The art of Kashida embroidery in Kashmir: A cultural revival story. Retrieved from https://www.thecitizen.in/index.php/en/newsdetail/index/14063/the-art-of-kashida-embroidery-in-kashmir-a-cultural-revival-story

Green Valley Treks and Tours. (n.d.). Green Valley Resort. Retrieved from http://www.greenvalleytreksandtours.com/green-valley-resort

Travel Setu. (n.d.). 5 Nights 6 Days Green Valley Kashmir. Retrieved from https://travelsetu.com/holiday-tour-packages/kashmir/5nights-6days/green-valley-kashmir/3637

Travelgar. (n.d.). Green Valley. Retrieved from https://travelgar.in/package/detail/amazing-kashmir-44852/green-valley-70367

Kashmir Mountain Adventure. (n.d.). About us. Retrieved from https://kashmirmountainadventure.com/about

The Tribune. (2023). Adventure tourism in Kashmir: A growing industry. Retrieved from https://www.tribuneindia.com/news/jammu-kashmir/adventure-tourism-in-kashmir-a-growing-industry-430723

Aulet, B. (2013). Disciplined entrepreneurship: 24 steps to a successful startup. Wiley.

Blank, S., & Dorf, B. (2012). The startup owner's manual: The step-by-step guide for building a great company. K&S Ranch.

Collins, J. (2001). Good to great: Why some companies make the leap… and others don't. HarperBusiness.

Fennell, D. A. (2014). Sustainable tourism: A global perspective (3rd ed.). Routledge.

Husain, I. (2005). The Himalayan irony: A study in Kashmir's economy. Sage Publications.

Howkins, J. (2001). The creative economy: How people make money from ideas. Penguin Books.

Kammerer, W. (Ed.). (2014). Cultural tourism in Asia. Springer.

Kawasaki, G. (2004). The art of the start: The time-tested, battle-hardened guide for anyone starting anything. Penguin.

Lyons, D. (2016). Disrupted: My misadventure in the start-up bubble. Hachette Books.

Norman, J. P. (2019). The AgriTech revolution: How agriculture is being transformed by technology. Wiley.

Osterwalder, A., & Pigneur, Y. (2010). Business model generation: A handbook for visionaries, game changers, and challengers. Wiley.

Pine, J. B., & Gilmore, J. H. (1999). The experience economy: Work is theatre & every business a stage. Harvard Business Press.

Amed, I. (2015). The business of fashion: Designing, manufacturing, and marketing fashion. Bloomsbury Publishing.

Barthes, R. (1983). The fashion system (R. Howard, Trans.). University of California Press.

Bussgang, J. (2010). Mastering the VC game: A venture capitalist's blueprint for starting and building a successful business. Penguin Group.

Christensen, C. M. (1997). The innovator's dilemma: When new technologies cause great firms to fail. Harvard Business Review Press.

Howkins, J. (2015). The creative economy: A new economic vision. Penguin.

Osterwalder, A., & Pigneur, Y. (2014). Value proposition design: How to create products and services customers want. Wiley.

Aaker, D. A., & McLoughlin, D. (2010). Strategic market management (9th ed.). Wiley.

Binns, J. (2014). The 10-day MBA: A step-by-step guide to mastering the skills taught in the world's top business schools. Three Rivers Press.

Cukier, W., & Snell, R. (2013). Developing successful entrepreneurship: Foundations of innovation, growth, and the future. Routledge.

Drucker, P. F. (2014). Innovation and entrepreneurship: Practice and principles. HarperBusiness.

Ghemawat, P. (2007). Redefining global strategy: Crossing borders in a world where differences still matter. Harvard Business Press.

Huggins, R., & Thompson, P. (2015). Entrepreneurship and innovation: A regional perspective. Routledge.

Khandwalla, P. N. (2012). The entrepreneurship environment: Technology, organizations, and strategy. Tata McGraw-Hill.

Kim, W. C., & Mauborgne, R. (2014). Blue ocean strategy: How to create uncontested market space and make the competition irrelevant (Expanded ed.). Harvard Business Review Press.

Porter, M. E. (1990). The competitive advantage of nations. Free Press.

Schilling, M. A. (2019). Strategic management of technological innovation (6th ed.). McGraw-Hill.

Taneja, S., & Toombs, L. A. (2014). Entrepreneurship in the global economy: New perspectives on research, policy, and practice. Routledge.

Zahra, S. A., & George, G. (2002). The net-enabled business innovation cycle and the globalization of entrepreneurship. International Journal of Entrepreneurship and Innovation Management, 2(3), 220-237. https://doi.org/10.1504/IJEIM.2002.002804

Pine, J. B., & Gilmore, J. H. (2011). The experience economy: Work is theatre & every business a stage (Updated ed.). Harvard Business Press.

Rogers, D. L. (2018). The digital transformation playbook: Rethink your business for the digital age (2nd ed.). Wharton Digital Press.

Southwick, S. M., & Charney, D. S. (2012). Resilience: The science of mastering life's greatest challenges. Cambridge University Press.

Teece, D. J. (2018). Business models and dynamic capabilities. Long Range Planning, 51(1), 40–49. https://doi.org/10.1016/j.lrp.2017.06.001

Visscher, A. (2017). Agribusiness: Principles of management. Pearson.

Rogers, D. L. (2016). The digital transformation playbook: Rethink your business for the digital age. Wharton Digital Press.

Schwab, K. (2016). The fourth industrial revolution. Crown Business.

Sinek, S. (2009). Start with why: How great leaders inspire everyone to take action. Penguin.

Siggelkow, N., & Terwiesch, C. (2019). Connected strategy: Building continuous customer relationships for competitive advantage. Harvard Business Review Press.

Southwick, S. M., & Charney, D. S. (2018). Resilience: The science of mastering life's greatest challenges. Cambridge University Press.

Heritage House. (n.d.). Cultural experiences in Kashmir. Retrieved from https://heritagehousekashmir.com

Greater Kashmir. (2023). Heritage House: Reviving Kashmiri culture through tourism. Retrieved from https://www.greaterkashmir.com/tourism/heritage-house-reviving-kashmiri-culture-through-tourism

TNAU Agritech Portal. (n.d.). Success stories of agripreneurs: Apple Doctor from Kashmir Valley. Retrieved from https://agritech.tnau.ac.in/farm_enterprises/pdf/MANAGE%20AGRL%20CLINIC%20Success.pdf

Greater Kashmir. (2023). Sabzar Nurseries: A model of agri-entrepreneurship in Budgam. Retrieved from https://www.greaterkashmir.com/business/sabzar-nurseries-a-model-of-agri-entrepreneurship-in-budgam

Kashmir Observer. (2024). Trout farming: A new wave of opportunity for youth in Kashmir. Retrieved from https://kashmirobserver.net/2024/01/15/trout-farming-a-new-wave-of-opportunity-for-youth-in-kashmir/

The Citizen. (2023). Young entrepreneur Mian Nazim transforms family orchard into a profitable agribusiness. Retrieved from https://www.thecitizen.in/news/young-entrepreneur-mian-nazim-transforms-family-orchard-into-a-profitable-agri-business

Jibran, S. (2024). Jammu & Kashmir: A rising hub for startups and innovation. Kashmir Observer. Retrieved from https://kashmirobserver.net/2024/09/30/jammu-kashmir-a-rising-hub-for-startups-and-innovation/